mood, he'd physically restrain me from leaving the room if he was in the middle of a really bad story.

"Don't be rude, Jason," he'd snarl, shoving me against a wall. "Now I'll have to start all over!"

I was careful not to complain to Mom and Dad when I wrote them. Since they weren't Christians I knew they wouldn't understand.

"We miss you, Jason," Mom usually added at the end of her letters. "Let us know if you want to join us."

"It is tempting," I told my friend Patrick. "There are some nights when I don't think I can stand it another second in my uncle's house."

"You mean you'd leave in the middle of your senior year?" Patrick asked, frowning.

"It's not that I want to leave," I explained, "but you just don't know what living with Kevin is like."

"I think you're doing okay," Patrick replied. "Better than okay, in fact."

That surprised me a little bit, because I had kept Patrick informed of exactly what was going on in my life and somehow expected him to be a little more sympathetic. "You really think living with that heathen cousin of mine is okay?" I demanded.

"All I know is that you used to miss church and Sunday school occasionally," he began. "Now you're there every week. And not just on Sundays either. I don't think you've missed a single Bible study or anything."

"No, of course not," I replied. "I get out of the house whenever possible."

"It's more than just getting out of the house," Patrick corrected. "Otherwise you'd go to the library instead of going to church. The library's a lot closer to your uncle's house."

"Yeah, but after being around Kevin, I need to be with my Christian friends," I said.

"Are you still having your devotions every night?" Patrick wanted to know.

I nodded. "Sure. Why?"

"Because when you were living at home you used to forget," Patrick reminded me. "How's your prayer life?"

"Never better," I admitted. "If I didn't have God to talk to, I think I'd go out of my mind. You know, it's funny, but when Kevin starts telling one of those dirty jokes of his, I start praying. It really works, too, because I haven't even heard him the last few times."

"I'm not surprised," Patrick told me. "This explains a lot of things."

I frowned. "Like what?"

"I couldn't figure out why you seemed to be growing as a Christian," Patrick answered. "After all the stuff you've been going through, I kind of expected you to get away from the Lord, but just the opposite has happened. And I'm not the only one who's noticed, either."

I shrugged. "Well, maybe so; I really hadn't thought about it. Of course I rely on God a lot more, but that's because I have to."

"You're just like Paul!" Patrick exclaimed suddenly. "Remember how his faith seemed to grow while he was in prison and suffering so much persecution? And not just Paul, either. Persecution and Christian growth seem to go together!"

I decided then that I would stick it out at Uncle Dan's house until June, no matter what. Either God could supply all my needs or He couldn't, and I had ample evidence that He could.

During those next few months I would pray like never before; but not only for myself, as I had been doing. I decided to pray for Uncle Dan and Aunt Caroline and Kevin—especially Kevin. He needed Jesus more than anybody else I knew.

It seemed like a lost cause, at times, but that Philippian jailer probably seemed like a lost cause, too, in Paul's day. God worked it out then; He could work it out now.

w w j d   p o w e r   s t a t e m e n t
It's easy to go through the motions of being a Christian. It's when we are up against some resistance though that our faith is strengthened. Dealing with persecution is rough, but it does teach us to rely on God, just like Jesus did.

s c r i p t u r e
You're blessed when your commitment to God provokes persecution. The persecution drives you even deeper into God's kingdom.
MATTHEW 5:10

The Professor

By Clint Baxter

Talk about dumb ideas! Our new youth director was full of 'em. I mean, if there was anybody in the whole youth group I couldn't stand, it was Craig Rimstead. So naturally we were assigned to the same prayer team.

To tell you the truth, I would've dropped out if my dad had let me.

"Do I have to go?" I asked that first Tuesday.

"Have to?" Dad repeated, frowning. "Isn't this the night you're starting prayer teams?"

"Uh huh." Prayer teams! I didn't even like the sound of it.

"Then I suggest you show a little more enthusiasm, Scott," Dad told me. "Prayer is a privilege."

"Look, Dad, I don't have anything against prayer," I began.

"Good," he said. "Get your jacket and I'll drop you off on my way to the post office."

There was no use arguing with my dad; I had learned that a million years ago. Most of the time I didn't mind too much—at least I had a father who cared enough to be strict—but this was different. If I didn't want to be on the same "prayer team" with Craig Rimstead, that should be the end of it.

It wasn't just Craig, though. I didn't like the whole idea of praying in a group. To me prayer was a very private thing and what I said to God was nobody else's business. I liked that verse about going into a closet and praying, but I guess Jim Collins had never read Matthew 6:6.

"The importance of prayer is grossly underrated by most Christians," Jim began the night he brought up the subject of prayer teams. "There's a lot more to it than rattling off a few memorized words before you eat or thanking God for getting you through the day as you doze off at night."

I couldn't argue with that. So what's your point? I wanted to know.

"At my last church we tried something which was quite successful," he continued. "It's based on Matthew 18:19 and 20. Tonight each of you will be assigned to a team of three and these teams will meet once a week for prayer. Naturally you can meet more often if you wish."

There was stunned silence. We all just sort of looked at each other. Admittedly there were a few people in the group I wouldn't have minded praying with. Cindy Daniels looked like a perfect prayer partner.

"When you came in this evening, you wrote your name on a slip of paper," Jim went on. "All those names are in this fish bowl and I'm going to pull out three at a time. Our first prayer session will be Tuesday night at 7:30."

He started reading the names. I just sat there and listened, hoping I'd be on the same team with somebody I liked.

"Josh Atwell, Jan Salter, and Cindy Daniels," Jim read.

Well, that takes care of Cindy, I thought, disappointed.

"Scott Reller," Jim read, pulling my name out of the fish bowl. "Bryce Colter," he continued. That was okay with me. Bryce was a friend. "And Craig Rimstead."

I nearly groaned. Not Craig! Anybody but Craig! Well, I'm just not showing up Tuesday night, I decided.

But of course I did. Bryce didn't come, so it was just Craig and me. *Well, one time won't hurt,* I thought.

"I believe I have located an excellent place for our team," Craig began in that sickening voice of his. No kidding, he always sounded like he was making a report when he talked. Some of the kids at school called him "The Professor," among other things. He wasn't very popular.

"I really don't know you very well, Scott," Craig went on, "so I'm glad we're on the same team. Maybe we should get acquainted before we start praying together. I think we should know when our fellow team members accepted Christ and a little about their families."

"Yeah, okay," I agreed halfheartedly. "I became a Christian when I was twelve. My parents are both Christians. Your turn."

"My father died when I was four," Craig began. "My mother had never worked before, but after that she got a job at the library so she could support my sister and me. I accepted Christ when I was six. Do you have any prayer requests, Scott?"

Just one, I thought. "Uh, no," I replied. "None that I can think of right now anyway."

"I know it's difficult because we don't know each other very well," he said, "but it's really quite essential that we learn to open up to each other during this prayer time each week. As it says in Galatians 6:2, we're to share our problems with our fellow believers."

My main problem is being here, I felt like telling him. "Well, I guess I could be doing better in school," I decided.

"Good," Craig answered, writing it down on a little pad. "I'm keeping track of our prayer requests. By the way, I wish you'd pray for a neighbor of mine. He really needs the Lord, but I can't seem to reach him."

"Yeah, okay," I agreed. "What's his name?"

"Danny Slagle."

I frowned. "Danny Slagle? You mean from school?"

"Yes. Do you know him?"

"Who doesn't! We've been friends for a long time. Well, sort of friends. He's about the last guy I'd expect to come to church, though."

"Will you pray first?" Craig asked.

I swallowed. "Well, okay. I'm not real big on praying out loud, though."

My prayer that first night was about the shortest on record. Oh, I prayed for Danny and asked God to help me get better grades, but the whole thing was over in about a minute.

Craig, on the other hand, went on and on and on. I thought he was going to pray all night. Sure, some of the things he said were good, but he could've kept it a lot shorter as far as I was concerned.

"I'm going to pray for you every day, Scott," he told me before we left that first night. "I hope you'll pray for me, too. I need help with my priorities. I spend so much time studying that I don't always have time for people."

I can believe that, I thought while I was waiting for Dad to pick me up. But at the same time, I kind of liked the fact that Craig had been honest enough to admit something like that. But he still prayed too long.

The first couple of weeks Dad had to prod me a little, but after that I started going because I wanted to. Not only was Craig my prayer partner, he also had agreed to help me with English and Algebra.

Praying with Craig every Tuesday night made me realize that he was okay underneath all that intellectual exterior. I mean he had feelings and needs and wants just like anybody else. Before long I was willing to share some fairly personal stuff with him.

I thought I knew how to pray before Jim started the prayer teams, but my prayer life really improved when I had someone to pray with on a regular basis. I also learned that prayer is a lot more than just asking for stuff. It made a big difference, that's for sure, and not just on Tuesday nights either, but even when I prayed alone in my bedroom.

And we began to see some results, too. Danny Slagle didn't suddenly show up at church and march down the aisle to receive Christ or anything, but he did agree to go to a sports night with me. And he had a good time too, even if he wouldn't admit it.

But the biggest changes that occurred happened within the youth group itself. A lot of kids—like Bryce, for example—had decided that prayer teams were dumb and so they just didn't show up on

Tuesday nights. But those of us who were faithful each week really began to grow. I wouldn't have believed it if it hadn't happened to me, but praying together on a regular basis can make all the difference in the world.

And if you don't believe me, just ask my good buddy Craig Rimstead!

w w j d   p o w e r   s t a t e m e n t

God wants us to bring every concern of our lives, big and small, to Him in prayer. He cares about each and every concern because He cares so much for us. Prayer doesn't always bring about the changes we want in our lives; but it does change us.

s c r i p t u r e

Pray all the time; thank God no matter what happens. This is the way God wants you who belong to Christ Jesus to live.

1 THESSALONIANS 5:17

The Queen

By Misti Chapman

"Hey, Jay just drove past the house again!" I shouted.

"Not so loud," my sister "Queen Gloria" commanded from her throne—otherwise known as the couch—where she was polishing her fingernails.

"But Jay—"

"As I've said before," Queen Gloria proclaimed, "Jay Watson doesn't interest me in the least, and just because he has been smitten by my great beauty in no way obligates me to grant his request for an audience, much less a date."

"I think I'm gonna be sick," I said, making a face. "And how do you know he even wants a date with you?"

"I suppose he's driving by to catch a glimpse of you?"

"No, of course not," I admitted. "But there is another girl who lives here."

"That's it!" Queen Gloria exclaimed. "He's one of Megan's!" She laughed uproariously at the idea.

"It would serve you right if he was," I told her as I stomped out of the room.

A moment later I came upon Megan, dressed in jeans and an old shirt, absorbed in her latest oil painting. I studied her, and the canvas. She was talented, there was no doubt about that, and not bad looking when she took the time to get herself fixed up. But she wasn't in Gloria's league.

While Megan was painting each afternoon, Gloria would perch on the couch and do her nails or read fashion magazines. She always sat in the same place, which just happened to be in front of the picture window. I started calling her "Queen Gloria" because of the regal way she sat.

It had begun when Jay Watson started coming to our church. He was a year older than Gloria and they had gone to junior high together. But he hadn't paid attention to her, despite the fact that she had a huge crush on him. Admittedly, Gloria didn't look her best in seventh grade. She had braces, pimples, and skinny legs.

But something happened during that year when Jay went to high school and Gloria finished junior high. Almost overnight she blossomed and became beautiful.

Right away boys started asking her for dates, but my parents wouldn't let her go out with anybody until she was fifteen, and then it was only with boys from the youth group.

Jay Watson was a member of the youth group, so that wasn't why Gloria pretended she wasn't interested. And he was a good looking guy, which was Gloria's specialty. No, it all went back to the way he had treated her in junior high. To make it even more insulting, he didn't remember her!

It was obvious from the beginning that Jay wanted to talk to Gloria. I was standing right there next to her that first night at youth group when he walked up to her. She had recognized him instantly, of course, and told Megan and me who he was.

Megan was on the refreshments committee and left for the kitchen before the meeting was over. I was in charge of putting away the chairs, but hadn't really started my job when Jay made his move.

"I'm Jay Watson and I—"

"Welcome to the group, Jay," Gloria interrupted coldly. "So nice to meet you. Now, if you'll excuse me—"

"Hey, wait a minute," Jay called after her, frowning. But it was too late, and Gloria was soon surrounded by her many admirers, not giving Jay a chance to say another word. If it had been me, I would've forgotten about her, no matter how pretty she was.

Not Jay. Before long he started driving past the house. Just once or twice a day in the beginning. Gloria pretended to be annoyed, but I knew better. She wasn't fixing herself up for me, after all.

One day he stopped in front of the house and got out of the car. Gloria was holding court in the living room, as usual, and she nearly went berserk when her mirror reflected the image of Jay Watson walking up the driveway.

"The nerve of him, not even calling first!" she exclaimed. "Well, if he thinks I'm available on such short notice. . . ."

The doorbell rang.

"Tell him I'm busy!" she ordered softly, heading for the staircase.

"Tell him yourself," I replied, disappearing into the kitchen.

"Kyle! Come back here!"

But I refused to obey. I was curious about how Queen Gloria would handle the situation, and there was no excuse for her not to open the door.

The bell rang again.

"Will somebody get that?" Megan called from upstairs.

She, Gloria, and I were the only ones home, so a moment later I heard the front door open. I sneaked into the dining room so I wouldn't miss a word.

"Hello, Jay," Gloria began.

"Well, hi! Do you live here too?"

"Too?" Gloria repeated. "Yes, I do. Who were you expecting?"

"Megan, of course."

That was too much for me, so I emerged from my hiding place. "Hi, Jay."

"Hi, Kyle. I'm finding out things about this family I didn't know before."

"Like what?" I asked.

"Well, I knew that you and Megan were related, but I didn't know Gloria was your sister too." He turned to Gloria and smiled. "I got your name right, didn't I?"

Gloria nodded blankly, almost as if in a trance. "Uh, I'll see what's keeping Megan. Excuse me." She ran up the stairs.

Jay looked after her. "That girl is always on the move!"

I frowned. "Were you serious—about not knowing Gloria lived here, I mean?"

"Sure. Why?"

"Because you drive past here all the time and Gloria usually sits in the front window."

Jay blushed. "You've seen me driving by, huh? I hoped nobody would notice, except Megan. But I didn't know who that was in the window. All I ever saw was the back of her head."

I could barely keep from laughing, but there were a few more things I had to get straight. "That first night at youth group you walked right up to Gloria," I began.

"Yeah," Jay agreed. "That second time too. I wanted to find out what had happened to the girl who was sitting next to her, but Gloria flew off without telling me. Finally I found out that it was Megan and she was fixing the refreshments. I got her address and phone number."

"You like Megan?"

"Sure. We talk on the phone a lot, and sometimes she waves to me from the upstairs window when I drive past!"

"Sorry to keep you waiting, Jay," Megan said as she descended the staircase looking prettier than I had seen her before.

I was standing at the picture window, watching them drive off together, when Gloria appeared at the top of the stairs. "Are they gone?"

"Yes."

"I always thought Megan had better taste than that."

I could've said something—a lot, in fact—but I didn't. Megan had gone off with Jay, and she was his first choice. That was quite enough for a queen to accept all in one day.

w w j d   p o w e r   s t a t e m e n t

A safe way to measure your own value is to see yourself as God sees you—no more but no less.

s c r i p t u r e

The stuck-up fall flat on their faces,
but down-to-earth people stand firm.

PROVERBS 11:2

Roi Lkc and Love

By Marlys G. Stapelbroek

I was pocketing the money from raking Mrs. Taylor's leaves when Mom called over the fence. "Wes? Mrs. Evan's new neighbors need a baby-sitter this afternoon. Are you interested?"

I was definitely interested in the money. I'd be sixteen next spring. When Randy Ericson graduated, I wanted to buy his '65 Mustang. But baby-sitting meant diapers. I wrinkled my nose.

"Rick gets out of school at three," Mom added.

"School?" So no diapers.

"And Mrs. Bradshaw pays $3.50 an hour."

"Three fifty?" Three was the going rate. I bicycled right over to the Bradshaws.

When I introduced myself, Mrs. Bradshaw gave me a huge smile. "What a Godsend," she said.

"Me?"

"Not many boys want to baby-sit," she explained, "but since my divorce, Rick needs male companionship." She sighed. "Each year it gets harder to find someone older."

I frowned. "Older than who?"

"Rick. He accepts authority better from someone older."

"Sure," I agreed, wondering what she was talking about. Of course, I was older.

Then I saw Rick. He looked about thirteen and almost my height, but his face was flat and his eyes slanted.

151

"Rick has Down's Syndrome," Mrs. Bradshaw explained quietly.

I swallowed. I wasn't even sure how to talk to someone like Rick. How was I going to baby-sit him?

I guess Mrs. Bradshaw understood because she murmured, "Rick needs the attention you'd give a child, but he craves the respect you'd show your friends."

I was still thinking about that when Rick held up the silver engine from a toy train toward me. "Engine," he announced.

Mrs. Bradshaw gave him a hug. "Why don't you and Wes set up your trains?"

Nodding, Rick laughed as cows spilled out of a green cattle car. He was unwrapping a red caboose when I realized Mrs. Bradshaw had left.

The train table was in the basement. Spreading out the track, we started hooking it up.

"Don't make the curves too tight," I warned. Rick's stubborn frown reminded me of his mom's advice, and I added, "If the curves are too tight, the train will tip over." His quick nod made me feel good, and a moment later he was looking for straight pieces, too.

After we finished the track, Rick emptied a box of toy buildings on the table. I sorted them into piles. "Houses, the school, a church—"

"God house," Rick corrected me, setting the white building in the middle of the table.

"God house," I agreed. It made as much sense as church.

The train was cruising through the model town when Mrs. Bradshaw returned. "It's time for Wes to leave," she told Rick, shaking her head at his protest. "I'm going to see if he can come again next week."

"Come next week," he told me, holding out his hand. I felt odd shaking it. He seemed like such a little kid.

Upstairs, Mrs. Bradshaw opened her purse. "I've never seen him take to someone so quickly. When I start work next Monday, I'll need a sitter after school." She handed me $7.00. "Would you be willing to come each day for a couple hours?"

Two hours a day, five days a week? At $35 a week? That wouldn't be enough to buy Randy's Mustang in June, but maybe I could make up the difference on weekends.

"Okay," I told her, pushing the money into my pocket. Playing trains after school wouldn't be so bad.

But Monday when Rick got off the school bus, he looked mad. Stomping into the kitchen, he threw a notebook page on the floor. "Can't make 'k,'" he shouted.

Picking up the paper, I studied the large, shaky letters. R-I-C, R-I-C. Again and again he'd tried making a "k," but the lines wouldn't meet in the middle.

"We could practice," I offered.

Snatching the paper out of my hand, he ran upstairs and slammed the door. I almost went after him, except I wouldn't chase a sulking friend.

Then I remembered the soccer ball downstairs. A few minutes later I was kicking it against the garage door. Smack, smack, smack. I was sure the rhythmic sound would break through Rick's sulk.

When I finally saw him in the kitchen doorway, I waved. "Come on," I called, gently kicking the ball toward him. With a shy grin, he ran down the steps and kicked it back.

We didn't work on his "k" that day or even the next, but eventually he let me help. It took a couple weeks, but when he finally showed his mom, Mrs. Bradshaw cried.

"I'm sorry," she sniffed, "but he's been trying to get 'k' for so long." I nodded, glad I'd helped make things click.

Over the weeks, we fell into a routine—soccer or the park on nice days, trains and coloring when it rained.

The first week of November, we had our first snow. I was trudging through dirty slush when I saw the sign in Lawson's Hardware Store. Hiring part-time for Christmas.

Pulling open the door, I found Mr. Lawson and asked for an application. "I only need one clerk," he explained. "It's just through Christmas and I pay minimum wage."

Minimum wage? That was over $5 an hour. "No problem," I told him, then headed for the Bradshaws.

I fixed Rick a peanut butter and jelly sandwich, then sat across from him at the kitchen table with my application. Name, address, and social security number were easy. Experience was harder, but I knew a lot about hardware from my odd jobs.

The real problem was Mr. Lawson's scribbled note at the bottom. Hours available. I couldn't work during school, and if I was with Rick afternoons, I needed evenings for homework. Mr. Lawson would never hire me if I could only work weekends.

I thought for a long time, but there was only one answer: I had to quit baby-sitting. Just through Christmas. Two months at the hardware store would give me a real shot at buying that Mustang. Mrs. Bradshaw would understand. And Rick—

He was coloring, drawing big letters.

"What are you doing?" I asked, puzzled.

He pointed to my application. "What you do."

Copying me. That's how he'd learned to make a "k" and head a soccer ball. But he'd written Roi Lkc.

"What are you writing?"

He sat up proudly. "My best words."

"Can you read them?" I asked, not wanting him to know I couldn't.

He pointed to Roi. "Trains and—" his finger slid over to Lkc "—God."

Trains and then God. I smiled, wondering how God felt about coming in second to a toy train. My smile faded. How would Rick feel about coming in second to a '65 Mustang? How could I throw away the trust and friendship we had for minimum wage?

Sighing, I picked up my pen and filled in my hours available—weekends. As I finished, Rick pointed to it.

"Your best word?"

I shook my head. "Not really." But what was my best word? How did I know God should come first and that Rick was miles ahead of an old Mustang?

Smiling, I realized there was one thing that put everything else in the right order. Reaching for one of Rick's crayons, I wrote in big red letters: Love.

wwjd power statement

Jesus always put people first. When there is a choice between better and best, you can always know that God wants you to choose to behave out of love for another person.

scripture

Self-sacrifice is the way, my way, to finding yourself, your true self. What kind of deal is it to get everything you want but lose yourself? What could you ever trade your soul for?

MATTHEW 16:26

Trusting

By Julie Durham

"Dad, can't we please stay up just a little while longer?" Michelle and Michael begged, their eyes full of pleading. "Please."

Uncle Doug smiled slightly but then he shook his head. "No, kids, for the last time, go to bed."

They pouted a little as they came and gave me and mom and dad hugs goodnight. "Hey, aren't you forgetting someone?" Doug asked as they started to drag out of the room. Still pouting, they gave him a hug and kiss and shuffled off to bed.

"They've grown so much, Doug." Mom said softly. "How do you do it?"

We hadn't really seen Michelle and Michael since they were only a year and two years old. At that time, Uncle Doug and Aunt Katie had moved to California. Since we live in New Hampshire, we didn't get together with them very often. After Aunt Katie died from cancer, Uncle Doug stayed out West for about a year. Then he decided to come back.

I was excited that Uncle Doug was back. He'd always been my favorite adult. I remember when he and Aunt Katie first had Michelle and Michael, I spent lots of time at their house. When I was afraid to talk to my parents about something, or they didn't seem to have time, I could always count on Uncle Doug and Aunt Katie to listen. Although we were heart-broken when Aunt Katie died, I was glad that Uncle Doug was coming home.

I'd hit it off with eight year old Michelle and nine year old Michael right away, even though I'm seventeen.

It wasn't that late. I didn't understand why Uncle Doug didn't let them stay up later—especially since it was their first night with us. But I soon forgot about it.

Since Uncle Doug only lives a couple of blocks from our house, Mom would watch the kids after school until Uncle Doug got home and I'd often go over on weekends to take them to the park or spend time with them. One day, I took some licorice with me to share with them. I was kind of surprised when Michelle grabbed hers and stuffed it into her pocket. Then she ran into the other room.

Michael started to tell me something, but Uncle Doug came into the room and I offered him a piece. He looked at me like he was trying to decide whether or not to say something.

"Julie, did you give a piece to Michelle?"

"Yeah, I did."

Uncle Doug sprinted through the other room and out into the back yard, with me and Michael close behind. He found Michelle hiding behind a bush.

"Okay, hand it over."

"What?" Michelle said looking innocent.

"You know what." He answered sternly. "Now."

Michelle scowled as she passed over the gummy, half-chewed licorice.

"You're mean," she announced, and began to cry. I didn't know what to do. From the baby-sitting I'd done, I knew never to butt in when parents were having a problem with their kids, but this was my cousin. And Uncle Doug was being awfully mean. What was the big deal about a lousy piece of licorice? Michelle looked at me and hurtled herself into my arms, sobbing like her heart was breaking.

Uncle Doug touched my shoulder. "Julie, I think you'd better go home for right now," he sighed. "I need to talk with the kids for a while."

"I was going to take them to the park . . . ," I started to explain.

"Thanks, but not today," Uncle Doug told me. I unwrapped my arms from Michelle and began walking away. "No, no, no. . . ." she screamed hysterically. I hesitantly looked back, but Uncle Doug had a hold of her hand and was leading her into the house.

Uncle Doug and the kids didn't come over that night, like normal. And I was afraid the kids were being punished because I took them licorice. I felt awful. All afternoon I thought about them and about Uncle Doug. He sure had changed. He seemed so strict—more than strict, he seemed mean.

I was moping about it all afternoon. Then Tony called. Tony Graziano. Dark skin, jet black hair, long black lashes, and clear blue eyes. Lately, Tony's been hanging around me at school. I don't know that he's a Christian. But as I told my best friend Pam when she mentioned something, I don't know for sure that he's not a Christian either.

Pam had frowned at me, "I think you have a good idea that he's not." I know the Scripture about being unequally yoked and everything. But it's not like I was planning to marry the guy. Who knows, maybe being around me will help him see that Christians aren't so bad. Maybe he'll even become one.

Tony and I talked for forty-five minutes before Mom made me get off the phone. Right before he hung up, he asked me to go to a picnic the next morning. "Sorry, I can't. Church." I told him. "I'd love a rain check though."

He didn't give me a hard time at all. That's one thing I liked about Tony. He's nice. Even nicer than all the Christian guys I knew—and a lot cuter than most. I mean, I figured that surely God doesn't want me to go out with a Christian guy when I can go out with a non-Christian guy who's nicer. After all, I'd been raised to believe that God wants the best for me. Tony doesn't drink or smoke or do drugs or even swear. And he's as moral as any Christian guy I know. And just like Tony didn't try to get me to skip church, I know he'd never resent my going to church, even if he doesn't go himself.

"How about next Saturday?" Tony asked.

"It's a date . . . er, an appointment," I answered with a smile and a bit of a blush—good thing he couldn't see me.

As I hung up the phone, Mom frowned. I knew she'd have fits about my plans to go out with Tony Saturday. I'd worry about that later in the week.

It was hard to sit through church Sunday— partially because I kept thinking, *I could be with Tony right now.*

And partially because the pastor was talking about obeying God—even when we didn't agree or understand. I quickly tuned him out and concentrated on Tony. I did feel another little flinch of guilt when we sang the closing hymn, *Trust and Obey,* but by the time we got home, I'd shrugged it off.

After supper on Monday, Mom handed me Michael's jeans and asked me to run them over to Uncle Doug's house. He'd ripped them at school and mom had patched them.

When Uncle Doug opened the door, he gave me a warm smile, "Julie! I just put the kids to bed, but come on in and have a Coke. It seems like forever since I've really talked with you."

We ended up sitting on the front porch swing, making small talk for a while. I told Uncle Doug a little bit about school, but I didn't mention Tony. I didn't want another lecture. Then Uncle Doug started talking about the kids.

"Julie, I know sometimes I must seem mean to you. Like Saturday. I didn't have a chance to explain, but Michelle's allergic to licorice. We've had a few scary times with her when she's eaten it.

"I know there are other times when I may seem too strict. Like making the kids go to bed early. I know when you were little your parents let you stay up. But you had a different temperament. You've always been a little bit of a night owl. Michelle and Michael aren't. If they're up past 8:30, they're at each others throats all the next day.

"Sometimes it's hard when I know other people think I'm being too strict or mean, but I do have a reason for every regulation I place on the kids."

I didn't know what to say, so I didn't say anything. He pushed the swing with his foot and continued.

"You've experienced it many times in your own life. Your parents tell you something and you don't understand their reasoning. But when your parents come down hard on you, it's because they love you and want to protect you. They know you don't always understand. And that hurts them almost as much as it makes you angry . . . parents hate it when their children just think they're being mean. But it's smart to obey them. Even when you don't understand."

Suddenly I remembered vague words I'd only half heard the pastor preach Sunday "When God gives a command it's usually for two reasons—because He wants to protect you and because He wants to provide for you—His way. When we disobey Him, we step out from under His umbrella of protection. And when we try to provide for ourselves instead of letting Him do it, we might miss the provision He had for us all along."

Sitting on Uncle Doug's front porch, enjoying the warmth of the early spring, I suddenly began to see God's command about not being unequally yoked in a new light. Maybe God was trying to protect me. And maybe if I stayed so set on Tony, I'd end up missing the provision that God has for me.

I knew I needed to do some thinking. Alone. As I walked down the street, the words floated back through my mind, "Trust and obey, for there's no other way to be happy in Jesus, but to trust and obey."

Mingling with the "enemy"—someone who wasn't on God's side of the battle—wasn't the only command

I'd broken lately. I needed to sit down with God and do some heavy-duty apologizing. But first, as I walked into the house, I walked straight to the phone. "Hello, Tony? I'm sorry, but about Saturday. . . ."

w w j d   p o w e r   s t a t e m e n t

God's commands for our lives are for one of two reasons: to protect us or to provide for us. When those limits seem restricting, remember that God is acting out of His love for us.

s c r i p t u r e

This is your Father you are dealing with, and he knows better than you what you need. With a God like this loving you, you can pray very simply.

MATTHEW 6:8

The New Neighbors

By Alan Cliburn

A big white moving van was parked in the Brewster's driveway when I got home from school that Wednesday. *So it really is true, after all,* I thought.

The Brewster's house had been empty for a while and we'd been hearing rumors that the family that was moving in didn't really belong in our neighborhood, if you know what I mean.

Of course just because that moving van was there didn't tell us anything about the new owners, I thought, standing on the front porch and watching the movers carry in a red couch. I could see they liked bright colors. But lots of people do; that didn't mean anything.

Before long a big car pulled up in front of the Brewster's house and my worst fears were realized. A whole family of them got out! There was a mother and father and three kids, including a guy about my age.

"Look at that fancy car," Dad said Saturday morning as he stood at the picture window. "Doesn't surprise me a bit!"

"Fred, it's no bigger than our car," Mom answered. "I'm going over to meet them this morning. Who's coming with me?"

"I-uh-I have chores to do," Dad replied quickly, heading for the garage.

"How about you, Kent?" Mom asked, looking at me.

I swallowed. It was bad enough having them in the neighborhood; did I actually have to go over there?

"I'm sure the boy will be attending your school," Mom went on. "He might already be enrolled, in fact."

"If nothing else, you can invite him to church," Mom said.

"Church?" I repeated, frowning. "You want me to invite him to our church? I thought they had their own churches!"

"Well, it's true that some churches do seem to be made up of members of one race," Mom admitted, "but all races are welcome at our church. Isn't Joe Wong in the youth choir?"

"Well, yeah," I agreed. Somehow that seemed different. Besides, Joe didn't live on my block.

Mom continued. "We know nothing of this family's religious background; we only know that their skin is a different color than ours."

Isn't that enough? I thought. But I shrugged. "Okay, I'll go. Let me put on a different shirt."

"Come right in!" the woman said after Mom introduced herself and me. "I'm Roxie Harris."

She was friendly and so was her husband, but that didn't mean anything. Anybody can act friendly, after all. The girls were kind of cute, I guess; probably about seven and ten, although it's hard to tell.

"And this is Chris," Mr. Harris announced as a tall, lanky guy about my age came into the room. He looked a little embarrassed.

"I'm Kent," I said, shaking hands with him. "Wanna come over and shoot some baskets later?" I heard myself ask.

"Yeah, that'd be great," he answered.

Chris was pretty good at basketball, which wasn't surprising, if you know what I mean. Actually we were pretty evenly matched, which made it fun. Chris wasn't loud or dirty talking or anything either, which caught me off guard. I guess you can't believe everything you hear.

"Would you like to go to church with me tomorrow?" I asked him before he went home. "We have a pretty good youth group."

"Is it okay?" he wanted to know.

"Sure, anybody can go to our church," I said before I realized how that sounded. "I mean, it doesn't matter what your church background is."

He smiled. "I knew what you meant. Yeah, I'd like to go."

And he went. I wasn't too sure how the other kids would treat him—some Christians are really prejudiced, if you can imagine such a thing—but nobody made any snide remarks; none that I heard anyway.

I thought Chris would only go that one time, but he really liked it and wanted to go back. In fact, his whole family went a couple of weeks later. Dad smiled and shook hands with Mr. Harris and all that, but I could tell it was killing him.

"We're thinking about joining your church," Chris told me one afternoon as we were walking home from school. "Have you heard any negative comments about our being there?"

"What do you mean?" I asked, feigning innocence.

He gave me a look. "You know what I mean! We're the only family of our race attending your church. Do you think it'll create any problems if we join?"

"It shouldn't," I replied. "I mean, the important thing at our church is a personal relationship with Jesus, not the color of someone's skin."

"Well, we are Christians," Chris assured me. "I accepted Jesus when I was nine."

I was sitting right up front the Sunday morning the Harris family joined our church. I knew there were some people, like my father, who weren't thrilled, but nobody said anything and Pastor Willis welcomed them warmly into our fellowship.

I wasn't home the day of the accident, but later Mom told me that Dad had fallen off the ladder while pruning some trees and gashed his arm really bad. It was Mr. Harris who drove Dad to the emergency room.

There's more. Despite Mr. Harris' fast work, Dad lost too much blood and needed a transfusion. Turned out he has some rare blood type and they couldn't find a donor. Mr. Harris volunteered to be tested and wound up giving Dad some of his blood!

"Well, we were brothers in Christ before," Mr. Harris told Dad one evening when the whole family was over for dinner. "Now we're blood brothers!"

"You probably saved my life," Dad said. "God brought your family into our neighborhood for a reason."

"We like it here," Mrs. Harris replied. "Thanks to you, we feel we really belong."

"If you guys are gonna get mushy about it, can Chris and I be excused?" I asked.

They laughed. "We're having dessert later," Mom reminded me.

"We'll be right outside," I promised.

Chris and I just sat on the front porch without saying anything for a while.

"I really am glad we moved here. I didn't want to at first. It was kind of scary moving into a minority neighborhood—you hear all kinds of stuff—but this is home now. Thanks for everything, Kent."

"That's okay," I told him. "For a white guy, you aren't so bad."

w w j d   p o w e r   s t a t e m e n t

Jesus sees us all the same. Remember that the person who may look different from you on the outside, is like you on the inside. He or she has the same hopes and fears, joy and hurt. It honors God when you choose not to make judgments about others based on their race.

s c r i p t u r e

Do as God does. After all, you are his dear children.
Let love be your guide. Christ loved us and
offered his life as a sacrifice that pleases God.

EPHESIANS 5:1-2 CEV

Emilio

By Dennis C. Gerig

Emilio stood at the end of the counter, polishing it for all he was worth. There wasn't a customer in the place and Mr. Reynolds had gone to the bank, but there he stood, working!

The other guys and I sat in a front booth, drinking free Cokes and talking about Emilio. They didn't like him much.

"What's he doing anyway?" Adam hissed. "Trying to make us look bad?"

Justin shrugged. "To who? There's nobody here but us. He'd be taking a break if he had any sense at all."

"So who says he has any sense?" Adam snickered.

Emilio glanced up self-consciously at the sound of Adam's snicker.

"Hey, there's the boss' car!" Adam exclaimed suddenly, pointing out the window. By the time Mr. Reynolds entered the restaurant a minute later we were all working. He glanced around and nodded approval.

It was a fast food restaurant with a dining room section for people who wanted to eat there, so the four of us were kept busy once the customers started coming in. Emilio really was a good worker, but that didn't matter to Adam and Justin. They hadn't even given him a chance.

Emilio had tried to fit in, being friendly and all that, but when he didn't get any encouragement he soon stopped trying, concentrating on his work. I felt sorry for him, but I couldn't do anything, not with Adam and Justin watching. They were friends of mine, after all.

169

"I need somebody to work tonight," Mr. Reynolds said one afternoon. "One of the girls on the night shift is sick. How about you, Scott?"

"No, I can't," I replied. "I have an appointment."

"Anybody interested in working tonight?" Mr. Reynolds asked.

"Not me," Adam decided.

"We got tickets to the ball game," Justin explained.

"I'll work," Emilio volunteered. "I don't mind."

Adam and Justin gave each other a disgusted look.

I would've worked that night, but I was taking a class at church, taught by the pastor. It was a class on witnessing, with a lot of on-the-job training. We usually went out in teams of three, with one experienced person as the leader and the other two as trainees. I was in the trainee stage.

"Most people are scared of witnessing and visiting people in their homes because they haven't done it before and are afraid of the unknown," Pastor Miller had explained the first week. "This course is designed to help you get over that fear."

It was a lot easier than I expected it to be. Most of our contacts were people who had visited the church, so they were usually glad to see us. After we invited them to come back to church and explained the various activities available, our leader shared the Gospel. Several people came to Christ as a result.

I kept hoping I'd learn how to share my faith well enough to tell Adam and Justin about the Lord, but considering the way they acted when I invited them to a youth group sports night I decided to wait a while. They just didn't seem at all interested.

"I thought of a way to get rid of Emilio," Adam whispered after Mr. Reynolds left for the bank and Emilio headed for the storeroom.

"How?" Justin questioned.

I didn't say anything.

"It's his turn to fill the salt and pepper shakers," Adam explained. "What if he puts sugar in the salt shakers?"

"All right!" Justin hissed.

I wanted to object, but I didn't. It wouldn't have done any good, after all.

Naturally there were lots of complaints from customers who were less than thrilled with sweet French fries.

"Who is responsible for this?" Mr. Reynolds demanded after the lunch crowd had thinned out.

"Emilio filled the shakers today," Adam announced.

"Yeah, I saw him," Justin chimed in.

"With salt," Emilio said, "not with sugar!"

"Take care of it," Mr. Reynolds told him. "Check every shaker."

"Yes, sir," Emilio agreed.

After that they played dirty tricks on Emilio whenever they could, like putting mustard in his change drawer.

"What is going on around here?" Mr. Reynolds wanted to know. I could tell he was really upset.

"My drawer was okay earlier," Emilio insisted.

"What do you know about this, Scott?" Mr. Reynolds asked.

"Me?" I replied. "I didn't see a thing!" It was true, but I probably wouldn't have told him even if I had seen Adam or Justin in action.

Eventually he quit, even though Mr. Reynolds tried to get him to stay on. "Accidents happen," he told Emilio.

Emilio shook his head. "There have been no accidents."

Adam and Justin thought it was great and spent most of their spare time congratulating each other. They liked the girl Mr. Reynolds hired to take Emilio's place, so everything ran pretty smoothly.

We were having good results in our witnessing class at church. "With all the teams we have now," the pastor said one night, "we have more than enough to handle the church visitors. So we're going to ask the more experienced teams to try going into a neighborhood and talking to whomever will let you in. Your assignments are on the table. Pray together and then be on your way."

My team was sent across town to an older section. I was really nervous, and left our packet of literature in the car.

"I'll go back for it," I said as we stood on the first porch.

When I returned, the door was open and the team was already inside. *That was fast!* I thought.

"Yes, I think I would be interested in visiting your church," I heard a familiar voice begin as I entered the house.

"Great!" my trainer responded. "One of our team members is in the youth group and will be glad to tell you about their activities. He should be back any—"

"Here I am," I interrupted. Then I froze. No wonder the voice sounded familiar! Facing me in that living room was Emilio! "Hi!" I began, extending a hand.

But Emilio did not take my hand. "You're from the same church?" he asked.

I swallowed. "Yes. Emilio—"

"It's a friendly church where we study the Bible," my trainer explained, obviously puzzled by the sudden change in Emilio's attitude.

"I would not be interested in attending your church," Emilio said. "You will excuse me now, please."

"Yes, of course," my trainer agreed, frowning. "May we give you some free literature—"

"No, thank you," Emilio said, walking to the door. "Good-bye."

"Emilio," I began. But the expression on his face convinced me that it was indeed time to leave. "I'm sorry," I managed on the way out. "But I'll be back."

"Don't bother," he told me.

I felt sick as we left that house. He treated me just as if I had been the one who did those terrible things to him at the restaurant! And I couldn't blame him.

I'd be back, though. I couldn't let him believe that my behavior and lack of courage was what being a Christian was all about.

w w j d   p o w e r   s t a t e m e n t
You have the power in every relationship in your life to draw others to or away from God.

s c r i p t u r e
Stay on good terms with each other, held together by love.
HEBREWS 13:1

The Unmasking

By Mike Chapman

Well, he's done it again, I told myself, glancing around to see if anybody else thought the youth director's latest idea was as dumb as I did. Of course from the back row it's pretty hard to see facial expressions.

"I know some of you came tonight expecting to see the video I've been telling you about for the past month," Dave went on.

"That's exactly why I came," I agreed.

"But I guess it got lost in the mail or something, because it hasn't arrived yet," he continued. "Maybe next week."

So why don't you just dismiss us and let us take off? I felt like asking. I didn't, of course. Lonnie Adams was sitting right next to me and he was a new Christian. I wasn't going to do anything to set a bad example for him. Not on purpose anyway.

"So this is the way it'll work tonight," Dave explained. "We're putting Galatians 6:2 into practice and we'll do it by breaking into small groups of about five each. Once you get your group organized, introduce yourselves around the circle and simply start sharing whatever's on your mind. Don't worry, we'll do it in stages."

Dumb! I thought. *Dumb! Dumb! Dumb!*

"Now there's a tendency to just share the good things the Lord has been doing in your life," Dave said. "That's okay for a couple minutes, but that verse in Galatians tells us to 'bear one another's burdens' and that means opening up to the others in your group, and taking off that protective mask most of us hide behind."

This whole idea is bothering me, I wanted to tell him.

"It's not easy, but it's scriptural and it will help you grow," Dave promised. "Okay, let's break into groups of five."

There was a lot of noise and confusion as the groups were formed. It would have been a good time to sneak out without being noticed, and I probably would have if Lonnie hadn't been there.

Since Lonnie and I were sitting right next to each other we just stayed where we were. Joe Fergus turned his chair around to join us and so did Claudia Reynolds and Diane Grossinger.

"Well, I guess we have our five," Joe announced.

Real good, Joe, I thought.

"One, two, three, four, five," Claudia counted.

I gotta get out of here! I told myself.

"Does everybody know everybody?" Diane asked.

We all looked at each other. I could hardly stand the excitement.

"I don't think I know you," Claudia decided, focusing on Lonnie.

Lonnie blushed. He blushes real easy—especially around girls.

"This is Lonnie Adams," I said. "Lives on my block."

"Oh yeah, you were in my English class last semester," Joe remembered.

"Do you have a sister named Gloria?" Diane questioned.

"No," Lonnie replied. "But I have a brother named Jeff."

"You're kidding!" Claudia exclaimed. "So do I!"

"Maybe you're related," I inserted.

Fortunately the youth director interrupted us before Claudia and Lonnie started climbing their family trees.

"Okay, you should have introduced yourselves by now," Dave said from up front. "The next step is to share something about yourself with the group."

Claudia told about getting a job and how that was an answer to prayer because there was a pink dress in the window of some store downtown that she just had to have. I thought I was gonna be sick.

"I've been a Christian for over three years!" Diane exclaimed.

"I've been a Christian for a month," Lonnie said, blushing.

Then they all looked at me. "How about you, Keith?" Claudia began.

"Everything's fine," I replied. "I'm a Christian and everything's great." I shrugged. "What else can I say?"

I didn't have to say anything else. Dave's voice rose above the rumble. "You should be finished sharing something about yourself," he told us. "And you probably know something about the people in your group that you didn't know before. Right?"

He was right about that, I had to admit. Pink dress!

"We're coming to the hard part," Dave went on. "I want you to go around the circle and tell something that is hurting you right now, spiritually or otherwise. Be open and honest."

There was mostly silence in the room for a few seconds, then spurts of embarrassed laughter.

"Well, I might as well start," Joe decided, swallowing.

I studied him. He was a big muscular guy, popular and all that. What kind of problems could he have?

"There's this new transfer from Colby High," he continued. "He plays quarterback, same as me, and he's good. The coach is talking about letting him start in the game against Taft. I have to admit that some of the feelings I've had toward that guy—and the coach—aren't very Christ-honoring, if you know what I mean. So I guess I could ask you guys to pray for me about my attitude."

"Well, my problem is with my sister," Claudia began. "She gets into everything I own and my parents act like she's an angel or something."

"Just a week ago we found out that my aunt has cancer," Diane said.

It was Lonnie's turn and for once he wasn't blushing. Well, not much anyway.

"I want my parents to become Christians," he managed, "my brother, too. So far they aren't interested."

That was all and then everybody was waiting for me to bare my soul. They could keep waiting, as far as I was concerned. I had an image to maintain, after all.

"Keith, you must have some hurt to share," Claudia said.

"Yeah, I got up in the middle of the night to get a drink and stubbed my toe," I admitted.

Nobody thought that was too funny.

"Everything's fine," I insisted.

"You mean nothing's bothering you?" Joe wanted to know. "You aren't having any trouble?"

"Well, things could be better at work," I confessed, getting mad just thinking about it. "My hours are being cut because the boss' nephew needs a job. It really isn't fair." I took a breath. It felt kind of good getting my feelings out in the open. That surprised me. "It must be sort of the way you feel about this new guy on the team," I told Joe.

All five of us just started talking about stuff then— well, I guess Lonnie mostly listened—and it was amazing how much we had in common. Maintaining a consistent prayer life and keeping up with devotions was hard for everybody in the group and we all had questioned our relationship with Christ at one time or another.

"Even you, Keith?" Diane asked.

"Even me," I admitted with a grin. I hadn't planned to open up the way I did, but it was sort of contagious. And once I got started it just seemed like the most natural thing in the world.

Praying in our little group was really a good experience, too. Claudia got a little carried away, but there was still something special about praying for people who had really shared their problems in such a personal way.

After youth group was over I began to wonder if I had said too much. I had been a Christian for a long time, after all. Joe and Claudia and Diane weren't exactly new Christians, either. What was a baby Christian like Lonnie going to think, hearing a bunch of supposedly mature believers admit that their lives weren't always so great?

"Too bad the video didn't come," I began as we walked home.

"I'm glad it didn't," Lonnie replied. "I was beginning to think something was wrong with me," he went on. "You and most of the other guys at church always go around acting like everything's fine and you don't have any problems or anything."

"Lonnie—"

"But I've had a lot of problems since I've accepted Christ," he continued. "Up until tonight I thought it was just me. So I'm glad that video didn't come and we got to talk."

"I guess I am too."

w w j d   p o w e r   s t a t e m e n t

A lot of people use sarcasm as humor or as a shield to protect themselves in an uncomfortable situation. The problem is that sometimes it can be hurtful or can detract from a meaningful experience for someone else.

s c r i p t u r e

Rash language cuts and maims,
but there is healing in the words of the wise.
PROVERBS 12:18

Metamorphosis

By Kent Phillips

It was the last place I wanted to be. I mean what guy wants to spend a perfectly good Monday night listening to some kids with questionable talent pound a piano?

But when your kid sister is playing in a recital and your strong-willed mother believes that the whole family should offer "moral support," you find yourself on the back row of the women's club. Period.

"What about dad?" I asked.

"Your father had to work late," Mom reminded me.

Miss Cathcart started the recital with her beginning students, which was fine with me. The songs were really short, and it was kind of funny when the little kids made a mistake or waved to their parents.

But as the kids got bigger, the songs got longer. I glanced at the program.

"Oh no, Martha Elizabeth Dunhill is next!" I hissed.

Mom gave me a threatening look and put a finger to her lips, so I didn't say what I was thinking. Of all Miss Cathcart's students, Martha Elizabeth was the absolute worst. She had been taking for years too.

Martha Elizabeth was no kid, by the way. She was about my age, and in fact we went to the same junior high. We weren't exactly friends, but we usually said "hi" when we passed each other in the hall.

As her fingers touched the keyboard, sour notes filled the air. No kidding, it was the worst-sounding stuff in the history of the universe.

"What's the name of this song anyway?" I asked.

Mom pointed to it in the program. "The Butterfly," she whispered. "By Grieg."

"Should've stayed in the cocoon!" I hissed.

"Not another word, Timothy!" Mom ordered, her face flushed.

But the kid sitting next to me on the other side had overheard what I said and giggled. "Should've stayed in the cocoon!" he repeated gleefully, snickering.

I tried not to laugh, so I snorted, which was even worse. That made the kid next to me laugh, out loud this time, and suddenly I lost it. I couldn't stop laughing, no matter how hard I tried.

At least not until Martha Elizabeth pounded her fists on the piano keys and stomped offstage. That had never happened before. I became very quiet very fast.

I don't know if my sister played well or not. I didn't even hear her, too wrapped up in my own thoughts and what Mom was going to do to me after the recital.

But she turned it around. "What are you going to do about this, Tim?" she wanted to know while we were waiting for Stephanie.

"Do about what?" I asked innocently.

"You've been a Christian long enough to know that what you did was wrong."

"Maybe I could pray for forgiveness?" I suggested hopefully.

"That's good," Mom agreed, "but it's not enough," Mom added.

I swallowed. "Uh, maybe I could apologize to Miss Cathcart?"

"And who else?" she wanted to know.

I looked at her. "Not Martha Elizabeth!"

"Think of all the money Mr. and Mrs. Dunhill have invested in piano lessons," she went on.

"Apologize to them, too?" I was feeling sick.

"Of course maybe your father can come up with some interesting alternatives," Mom continued.

"I'll apologize," I decided quickly.

Well, might as well get it over with, I told myself the next day at school.

"Timothy!" she said when I walked up to Martha Elizabeth before school. "I was hoping I'd see you today!"

I cleared my throat. "You probably want to talk about last night, huh? Look, Martha Elizabeth—"

"Thanks for saying what you said," Martha Elizabeth interrupted.

I listened for sarcasm. There was none. "You were glad I smarted off?" I asked. "But—"

"Oh, my parents were upset by what you said and what I did, but it worked out great," Martha Elizabeth assured me. "I've been wanting to quit piano lessons for a long time and last night they finally realized that their daughter is not going to become a famous concert pianist. I'm going to study art—I may actually have some talent for it!"

I looked at her. I had known Martha Elizabeth for a long time without ever realizing how pretty she was.

"Uh, what are you doing at noon, Martha Elizabeth?" I heard myself ask.

"Eating lunch," she replied with a giggle. "Why? And call me Marti. I dropped the Martha Elizabeth a long time ago, even if Miss Cathcart still put it in her recital programs that way."

"I-uh-I thought maybe we could have lunch together," I went on, blushing, "you know, in the cafeteria."

"I owe you a lot for rescuing me from piano lessons, Timothy."

"Tim," I corrected in my deepest voice.

The bell rang then and we started off toward first period together. Mom wanted a full report on my apology to Martha Elizabeth—I mean Marti. She'd get one, all right, but it would be edited!

I had never asked a girl to eat lunch with me before, or do anything else, for that matter. Maybe it took a butterfly to get me out of my cocoon!

w w j d   p o w e r   s t a t e m e n t

Self-control is another one of the fruits of God's spirit at work in our lives. When we faithfully seek Him and spend time in His word and in prayer, the fruit of self-control will begin to show.

s c r i p t u r e

God's Spirit makes us loving, happy, peaceful, patient, kind, good, faithful, gentle, and self-controlled. There is no law against behaving in any of these ways.
GALATIANS 5:22-23 CEV

My Cousin's Secret Weapon

By Clint Baxter

My name wasn't on the list. I guess I could've lived with that, except for one thing. Brent's name was right up there at the top. He had done it to me again.

I hardly knew my cousin until his dad—my uncle —was transferred out here a year ago. At first Brent and I got along okay, but it soon became apparent that he was better at stuff than I was.

There were no jobs available, but he found one anyway.

"Where?" I had wanted to know.

"Food World."

I stared at him. It was just around the corner, a lot closer to my house than his. "You're kidding!"

But he wasn't, of course. Brent always managed to make things come out his way. I figured he had a secret weapon.

He was a good student too. After the first semester I tried to make sure that Brent and I weren't in the same classes. It wasn't always possible. We both wound up taking Mrs. Hobson for English. I didn't mind. English was one subject that always came easily for me.

Unfortunately Mrs. Hobson decided that English included spoken language as well as written language.

"Each of you will prepare a five-minute speech," she announced early in the semester.

Mrs. Hobson advised us to talk about something we knew about, so I chose photography. I thought I knew a lot about it, but when I got up to give my speech, I froze. What came out of my mouth was mostly dull facts about shutter speed and types of film that nearly put the whole class to sleep.

Nobody expected too much when Brent got up to talk about his butterfly collection, but within a minute he had everyone roaring with laughter—me included. In five short minutes he had not only enlightened us with a lot of stuff we didn't know about butterflies, but he had entertained us at the same time. Miss Hobson was so entertained she gave him an A; I got a C.

Basketball was something else, though. This was going to be the year I made the team.

"I hear you're going out for basketball," Brent said one afternoon.

"Yeah, I am."

"Me, too."

"Good." I wasn't overly enthusiastic, but it didn't bother me. I was slightly taller than Brent. Besides I had seen him play in gym class a few months earlier. He was only fair.

"Want me to pick you up for that thing at church tonight?" he questioned.

I frowned. "What thing?"

"You know, that inner-city project."

"Uh no, I won't be able to go—too much homework."

Also I thought it sounded like a rotten idea. Our youth pastor decided that we should go down to this housing development one night a week, get to know some of the kids, and tutor them on a one-to-one basis.

I went the first night and it was a real mess. Those inner-city kids were rowdy and didn't seem one bit impressed that we had given up an entire evening to help them out. I had no intention of going back.

"By the way, Dave tells me that Brent is trying out for the basketball team," Dad began one night. "How about you, Ryan?"

"Yeah, I am," I assured him.

"Want to shoot a few baskets after supper?"

"Thanks, but I'm kind of tired tonight," I decided. It was nice of Dad to offer, but I played basketball at school all the time; I was definitely ready for the tryouts.

Or at least I thought I was. The coach lined us up and let us take ten free throws first. I made six out of ten, which was pretty good, but some of the other guys were making eight or nine out of ten, including my cousin. When did he get so good? What was his secret weapon anyway?

"I'll post a list of the guys who made it on the bulletin board Monday afternoon," Coach Larson told us an hour later. "Thanks a lot for coming out."

Of course my name wasn't on the list and Brent's was. And to make matters worse, that was the day when he was coming to stay with us for a few days while his parents were out of town. I couldn't even escape him at home!

"Congratulations on making the team," I forced myself to say when I entered the house and saw him sitting at the kitchen table.

"Thanks, Ryan," he replied. "You'll make it next time. Want to shoot a few baskets?"

"No thanks," I said. "Have to write my outline for that speech Mrs. Hobson assigned us."

I went up to my room, but it was a little hard to concentrate with the basketball thumping against the garage door every couple of seconds.

"Now I know what your Aunt Margaret meant," Mom said suddenly, entering the room with some clean T-shirts.

I frowned. "About what?"

"Brent's basketball workouts," Mom explained. "According to Margaret he shoots baskets for hours every day."

I nodded. *No wonder he was so good,* I thought. I really hadn't spent much time practicing at all, not by comparison.

He excused himself right after supper and went up to his room. Walking past the door later I heard him talking. I listened. If that was his speech it didn't sound very funny, and he stumbled around for words too.

An hour or two later, after watching some television, I went past the room again. *Brent was still practicing, only it seemed a lot smoother than before,* I thought, frowning. I planned to read mine over a couple times—once I thought of a topic—and let it go.

The phone rang just as I was sitting down at my desk. It was the youth pastor. "Ryan, we need more people involved in our inner-city project. How about it?"

"Well," I began.

"Brent's probably told you about the boy he's been tutoring," Mr. Reynolds went on. "Cordell prayed to receive Christ last week," the youth pastor continued. "Several kids have, in fact. It's been kind of hard, but we're starting to see results. Pray about it, Ryan."

"Yeah, I will," I promised half-heartedly. *Just because Brent led some kid to Christ didn't mean I could*, I thought, passing the guest room again.

I heard his voice, so I listened. He was still going over his speech! I couldn't believe that guy! *And he'll probably get another A*, I thought disgustedly. *If I spent that much time on mine I could get an A, too.*

So why don't you? I asked myself.

Who has the time? I answered.

You do! And you probably would've made the basketball team if you had put in enough time working out! You might've even got that job at Food World if you had hung in there instead of deciding you didn't have a chance!

I frowned. Was that the real difference between Brent and me? He was willing to put in the extra time and energy to get what he wanted and I wasn't?

I was still standing there when Mom's voice came up the stairs. "Ryan, that special you wanted to see is coming on."

I started for the staircase, then stopped. "Thanks, but I have too much homework, Mom." It would be hard to change some of my priorities, but change them I would. My cousin needed a little competition!

wwjd power statement

Self-discipline is a a fruit of God's spirit and a sign of self-care.
If you care about yourself, you will take care of the concerns of
your life, your responsibilities, reputation, and testimony.

scripture

So prepare your minds for service and have
self-control. . . . In the past you did not understand,
so you did the evil things you wanted. Be holy in
all you do, just as God . . . is holy.

1 PETER 1:13-15 NCV

Shattered Dreams

By Al Burns

I couldn't even close the screen door quietly. It banged shut, announcing my arrival.

"That you, Rob?" Mom called from the kitchen.

"It's me," I replied, heading for my room. All I wanted to do was be alone.

She appeared in the doorway. "Supper won't be ready for two hours."

I felt like telling her, in no uncertain terms, that I probably wouldn't feel like eating supper later, but I didn't. She'd just ask what was wrong and I'd tell her and she'd try to cheer me up and I couldn't handle that at the moment.

"It's been a rough day," I added. "Think I'll lie down for a while."

I stretched out across the bed, hoping that sleep would come instantly, giving me some relief from my depression. *It's your own fault,* I told myself. *It was stupid to try out for the team.*

Personally I thought I had a chance this time. I gave it my best shot, just as I had when I tried out for the track team, the football team, and the basketball team. When I came in dead last during track tryouts I knew I was finished, and I was admittedly too small for football and too short for basketball. But tennis?

True, about half of my serves went into the net; but I did manage to return a few serves. Some of the other guys weren't much better.

Let me make it, Lord, and I'll give You all the credit, I had prayed as I walked toward the bulletin board outside the coach's office.

I studied that list for a couple of minutes, almost like I expected my name suddenly to appear. But it hadn't, of course. Another dream shattered.

Why, God? I asked as I lay across the bed. He had to know how much I liked sports. Suddenly there was a knock at my bedroom door. "Rob, are you asleep?" Mom's voice asked.

I wanted to be, but I wasn't. "No, Mom," I replied, sitting up. "Come on in."

She opened the door. "I hate to bother you," she said, "but I made cookies this afternoon. Would you mind taking some to that new family at the end of the block?"

I did mind, but I stood up. "I'll take them."

"I believe they have a boy around your age," she went on.

I wasn't in the mood to be social, but I could go through the motions. *Maybe nobody will be home,* I thought.

But a nice-looking lady came to the door right away. I introduced myself and told her why I was there.

"How nice!" she exclaimed, taking the cookies. "Tell your mother how much I appreciate this!"

"I will," I promised.

"You must meet my son," she continued. "Just a second, please."

The coach could've put me on the second team, I told myself as I was waiting.

"I'm sorry," our new neighbor announced suddenly. "Marc's asleep. I know he'll want to meet you, though. Please stop by again. And don't forget to thank your mother for the cookies," she called.

I nodded. Mom knew how to make good cookies, all right. In fact, she had a talent for cooking. My sister's talent was music, and Dad could fix just about anything.

And then there's me, I thought. *Mr. No Talent.*

"Hi, Rob!" one of the kids in the neighborhood yelled suddenly. "We were playing doubles till Scott had to go home. Will you fill in? We've got an extra racket."

"No thanks," I replied. *Besides, haven't you heard? I* felt like adding. *I'm no good at tennis; just ask the coach!*

I went home and relayed the new neighbor's undying gratitude to my mother for her cookies.

"You had a call while you were out," Mom went on.

I frowned. I didn't get many calls. "From whom?"

"Somebody from the church," she said. "Volleyball practice will be tomorrow night."

Not that I had any intention of going. I was giving up sports. Well, maybe it was the other way around. They had given me up and I might as well face the fact that I was no athlete.

Mom was waiting for me when I got home from school the next day. "Mrs. Talbott just called," she began.

I looked at her. "Mrs. Who?"

"Our new neighbor," she explained. "Marc is anxious to meet you."

I wasn't especially anxious to meet him. The newly formed tennis team had started workouts that afternoon.

Five minutes later I was following Mrs. Talbott down the hall to Marc's room. I wanted to ask why he didn't just come out and meet me in the living room, but I kept my mouth shut.

I found out for myself. Lying in a hospital bed was a guy about my age. He smiled when I entered the room and stuck out a hand. "Hi, I'm Marc Talbott," he said.

"Rob Winslow," I replied.

It didn't take long to discover that Marc was paralyzed from the waist down, the result of a bicycle accident a year earlier. He was very open about it and seemed to accept the situation.

"There is a slight chance that I'll walk again," he added, "but I'm leaving that in God's hands."

"Are you a Christian?" I asked. "So am I!"

"Yeah, I don't know how I would've handled this if it weren't for the strength that God has given me," Marc said. "I went through a period of bitterness and all that, but my pastor stuck with me and helped me understand that verses like Romans 8:28 are either true or they aren't."

I didn't answer.

"I must've heard that verse about being content regardless of the circumstances a million times," Marc went on. "But the more I thought about it, the more I realized that I could easily have been killed in that accident and that God kept me alive for a reason."

I didn't know what to say.

"I was planning to become a professional football player," Marc continued, "so after the accident I figured my future was shot. 'Try something else,' my pastor kept telling me."

"And did you?" I asked.

"Yeah, I tried painting, but when Mom said she liked my horse picture I knew my career as an artist was limited."

I frowned. "How come?"

"It was supposed to be a dog!" Marc exclaimed with a grin. "Then the pastor suggested I try writing my story. I did and writing came really easy for me. I've sold several short stories and now I'm working on a book. I still like football and hope to do some coaching someday," Marc said. "Just because I can't play doesn't mean I can't enjoy the game, after all." He looked at me. "Are you into sports at all, Rob?"

"A little bit," I heard myself reply. "I'm not good enough for the varsity teams at school or anything, but there's a church volleyball team I might play on."

"Hope I can get to one of the games sometime," Marc answered.

I thought about Marc as I walked home a little later. Paralyzed, and he was still trusting God and looking to the future. And I was all upset because I hadn't made the tennis team at school!

Okay, so maybe I wasn't so great at sports. So what? God obviously had something else planned for me. Wasn't that enough?

"Rob, can you play?" the same kid who had asked me the day before yelled.

I started to say "no," but glanced back at the Talbott house and nodded my head. I had two arms and two legs that still functioned. It was the least I could do.

wwjd power statement

It's not hard to look at what others have and feel sorry for yourself for what you lack. But God gives abilities, talents, and opportunities to each of us and expects us to use them wisely.

scripture

Then you will say to the Lord, "You are my fortress, my place of safety; you are my God, and I trust you."

PSALM 91:2 CEV

The Weekend I'll Never Forget

By Cindy Wainwright

My father, who will be forty-three in May, acted like a little kid when the official notice arrived. "I made it!" he announced triumphantly, waving the letter and almost jumping up and down. "I'm the new regional manager!"

"That's real nice, Daddy," I added from the breakfast table where I was having a bowl of cereal.

"And listen to this," he went on, still about two feet off the ground. "Your presence is requested at the executive officers' annual meeting next weekend in San Francisco. All expenses will be paid by the company, and your wife is cordially invited to accompany you."

"San Francisco?" Mom echoed, breathlessly. "Oh Stan, we haven't been there since our honeymoon!"

"Wow, that really is nice," I agreed. "Too bad it's only for two!"

"I hadn't thought of that," Mom replied quickly, a frown working its way across her forehead. Dad just smiled absently in my direction, still excited about his new appointment.

"I was only kidding!" I told Mom "I don't want to go. I can't. I have a date with Darryl on Saturday."

It turned out that my wanting to go along wasn't the part that concerned her. "We can't go off and leave Carla home alone," she began. "Stan! Are you listening?"

"What's that?" Daddy asked, reading his letter for about the fiftieth time.

"Mother, I'm nearly seventeen!" I reminded her.

"What's wrong?" Daddy wanted to know.

"Stan, put down that letter and listen!" Mom exclaimed. "What will we do with Carla next weekend if we go to San Francisco?"

"There's no 'if' about it," Dad corrected firmly. "We're going, all right. I've waited five years for this promotion and I want you there with me, Lois."

Mom was undeniably pleased, even though there was still concern in her eyes. "But what about Carla?"

"I think you're underestimating our daughter," Daddy answered, looking at me in a special way. "She's no longer a child, you know. She's a young woman, and I believe she's more than capable of managing her own life for one weekend."

"Thank you, Daddy," I said. "I appreciate your trust."

"It has nothing to do with trust," Mom insisted. "It just isn't safe. I was reading a story in the paper about a—"

"Oh Mother!" I interrupted, hoping Daddy would come to my rescue.

But he didn't. "Your mother's right," he said. "I'd rather you didn't stay alone. Why don't you ask a girl friend to spend the weekend?"

"I'll ask Mandy," I replied.

I called Mandy and gave her the full rundown. "It's okay," she told me a moment later. "At least for Friday night. I'm not sure about Saturday, though. Sometimes I baby-sit for the Reinharts on Saturdays. I won't know until the middle of the week."

I hung up and went to tell my parents.

"She can stay both nights?" Mom asked.

For a second I almost said "yes," but somehow I couldn't. "Probably," I replied. Then I explained about the baby-sitting job.

"But suppose the Reinharts need her for Saturday night?" Mom questioned.

"Then I'll just ask someone else," I said simply.

That seemed to satisfy Mom, so we didn't discuss it after that.

We hadn't dated much, but I liked Darryl a lot more than I wanted him to know, and my stomach always felt kind of fluttery when I was near him.

"What have you heard from Mandy?" Mom asked Thursday night.

"She's planning to come over about seven tomorrow evening," I replied.

"What about Saturday?"

"Mrs. Reinhart hasn't called, so she's planning to spend Saturday night here, too," I said. "She's going out, but so am I. Neither one of us is planning to stay out late, though."

At five o'clock the next afternoon, Mom and Daddy were ready to leave for the airport.

"Have a good time."

"We will honey," Daddy promised. "Your mother and I will be able to enjoy this trip more completely than some parents because we have absolute faith and trust in you. That means a lot to us."

"It means a lot to me, too, Daddy," I managed, swallowing. "You'd better go now or you'll miss the plane."

Mandy arrived at seven and we watched television for a while. Fortunately Mandy and I had been friends for so long that I didn't have to entertain her. She even brought her books along and did some homework.

We slept late the next morning and were having a leisurely breakfast when the phone rang. It was Mom, just checking to see if everything was okay. I assured her that everything was fine.

I had no sooner hung up when the phone rang again. This time it was for Mandy.

"Mrs. Reinhart?" she repeated, frowning and looking at me. "Tonight? Well, I guess it'll be all right."

"Are you baby-sitting tonight, after all?" I asked.

"Yes," Mandy replied, making a face. "It's one of those last minute deals that I hate, but if I turn them down they're liable to get somebody else permanently."

"But I thought you had plans," I reminded her.

"It was nothing definite," she explained. "The youth group is going out and Tom Patterson asked if I was going. I told him I would be if I didn't get a baby-sitting job. He'll understand."

"I hope my parents will," I said.

"What do you mean?"

"They think you're spending the night here."

"I still can," Mandy replied. "The Reinharts hardly ever stay out past midnight. I'll have him drop me by here instead of going home—that is, if you'll be back by then!"

"Darryl knows I have to be in by eleven."

Darryl picked me up at seven-thirty and we went to a basketball game. I wasn't wild about sports, but it was apparent that Darryl was. So I showed as much enthusiasm as possible.

After the game we went out to get something to eat and then home. There was something about being with Darryl that made the time fly by. I could hardly believe it was nearly eleven.

"I remember what your dad told me about your curfew the first time I took you out," Darryl said. "And I like to stay in good with dads! Where is he tonight, by the way?"

I explained about Dad's promotion and the weekend in San Francisco. "Mom called this morning." We got out of his car and walked to the porch together.

"You mean you're home all alone?" he asked.

"No, they didn't want me to stay alone, so my friend Mandy is staying with me," I corrected. "But she is baby-sitting tonight." I fished the key out of my purse and inserted it in the lock.

"Maybe I'll come in for a minute," he suggested.

"Well, I don't know," I replied. I wanted him to, but I wasn't sure if my parents would approve.

"I really should check the place out," he went on. "You know, to make sure nobody's in there."

We went from room to room together, Darryl looking inside closets and under beds. I felt very safe with him next to me.

"Well, nobody's here," he announced.

"Thanks—"

Suddenly I was in his arms and he was kissing me—hard. At first I tried to break away, then I just relaxed and kissed him back. Again and again and again.

"Darryl, we shouldn't," I told him finally, gasping.

"Why not?" he whispered. "We're alone and nobody'll know. I really like you, Carla."

"I like you, too," I admitted, "but—"

"But nothing," he interrupted gently.

I had often wondered what I would do if a guy pressured me about sex. I had been convinced that I could handle myself in any situation. But that wasn't how I felt as Darryl held me close. My heart was pounding and I knew I was weakening.

"Your parents won't be back until tomorrow night," he reminded me, "and they were the ones who didn't want you to be alone!"

He said it as a joke, almost as if deceiving parents was something to be proud of. I remembered what my father had told me before he and Mom left for the airport. He trusted me, and I had no interest in betraying that trust.

"You'd better go now," I managed as firmly as possible.

"Carla—"

"Now."

I was standing in the open door, watching as Darryl drove off and puzzled by his casual attitude about sex—almost as if it didn't really matter and he was just seeing if I would give in—when another car stopped at the curb and Mandy got out.

We had been friends for years, but I was never quite so glad to see her as I was right then.

"What's wrong?" she asked when she reached me.

"Come in and I'll tell you," I answered. "I'll never forget this weekend!"

w w j d   p o w e r   s t a t e m e n t

Remember two key principals about dealing with sexual pressure. 1. Decide ahead of time that you will make decisions about your sexual behavior based on God's word, not on how you feel. 2. Make every effort to stay out of situations where your convictions might be compromised.

s c r i p t u r e

So run away from sexual sin. Every other sin people do is outside their bodies, but those who sin sexually sin against their own bodies.

1 CORINTHIANS 6:18 NCV

Foolproof

By Alan Cliburn

It was Tuesday afternoon and we were heading back to the warehouse, Joel and me. I couldn't believe I was actually getting paid good money just to drive around town, but I wasn't complaining either. There was more than driving involved, of course. Joel and I delivered orders for Office Warehouse, which included furniture like desks and filing cabinets.

On this particular Tuesday the truck was in the shop, so Mr. Kramer let us take one of the company cars. Fortunately there was no furniture to deliver, just packages. One of us could have handled it easily, but Mr. Kramer wanted us both to go.

"Might as well start learning how to do the paperwork, Sam," he told me before we left the warehouse.

The paperwork was a piece of cake. We just had to get somebody to sign for the merchandise at every stop. We had several deliveries in the same vicinity. Maybe that's why we finished so soon.

"Hey, turn left at the next corner," Joel said suddenly.

"We've worked hard enough for one afternoon," he went on." Let's take a little break. Pull up there in front of Harry's." Harry's was a "family recreational center," with video and computer games and stuff like that.

"Are you kidding?" I replied. "We have to get back to the store. Mr. Kramer knows we didn't have a lot of deliveries. Besides. . . ."

"Relax," Joel interrupted. "I mean, will you just trust me to work it out? I guarantee that it'll be okay."

203

He opened the door and got out, but I just sat there behind the steering wheel. Joel was always working the angles and so far he hadn't gotten caught. This was different, though. This time he was asking me to go along with him.

"Are you coming or not?" he demanded.

"I don't know," I answered. "It doesn't seem right."

"Don't be wound up so tight," he advised. "Or is having fun against your religion?"

For a second I nearly wished I hadn't opened my mouth to Joel about my faith, but I had. "I just believe in giving a guy his money's worth and Mr. Kramer isn't paying me to play."

"Kramer won't know anything about it," Joel hissed, leaning through the window on his side of the car. "What's the matter, can't you Christians do anything?"

That just about did it. The last thing I wanted was to give Joel a negative impression of being a Christian, but at the same time I wasn't quite dumb enough to give in. Still, I was tempted. "What'll we tell Mr. Kramer if we get back an hour late?"

Joel grinned. "We had a flat tire!"

"Yeah, but we didn't. Besides, he'll want to see a receipt if we got it repaired."

"We didn't get it repaired," Joel informed me. "We just put on the spare ourselves. We had some trouble with the jack, that's why it took so long. It's foolproof! Come on."

I knew I'd never get through to Joel if he thought Christianity was nothing but rules and regulations. I could make up the extra time at the warehouse later and he'd never know the difference. But something told me it was still wrong, regardless of how much rationalizing I did.

"I'm going back to work, Joel," I heard myself say.

"Don't be a jerk all your life," he began.

I answered him by starting the motor. I guess he knew I wasn't kidding, because he got in, slamming the door shut behind him. "I won't forget this, Turner," he snapped.

"You guys are back early," Rex Keller said as I parked the car. He ran the loading dock for Mr. Kramer.

"Yeah, we are," Joel agreed, giving me a nasty look.

"It was a light load," I added, ignoring Joel.

"We can use some help inside," Rex went on.

"Thanks to you, we'll be working in that hot warehouse all afternoon when we could be at Harry's," Joel hissed.

Joel wasn't kidding about the warehouse. It was like an oven, with little ventilation. Admittedly I had second thoughts about my decision as perspiration started running off my body a few minutes later. Joel kept his distance too, working at the other end of the building. Up until that day we had gotten along pretty well, despite our differences.

"Joel, Sam, I'd like to see you in the office," Mr. Kramer announced suddenly. It was cool in his office. I could have sat there for the rest of the day! "Was there some reason why you didn't turn in your routing sheet, Joel?" Mr. Kramer asked.

Joel gave me a superior, amused look. "Sam was in charge of the paperwork today," he replied.

"Oh no!" I groaned. "Left it in the car! Be right back." I stood up and headed for the door.

"You can get it later," Mr. Kramer assured me. "Have a seat, Sam. I really called you in here to commend you for the work you've both been doing lately. I've gotten nothing but good reports from customers for your fast, courteous service."

"Thanks a lot," I said.

"Yeah, thanks," Joel added.

"A job of this type requires men who are trustworthy," Mr. Kramer continued. "Once you leave the store you're pretty much on your own. Unfortunately not everyone can handle this kind of freedom and I was admittedly apprehensive about hiring guys your age." Joel and I just sat there.

"No more," Mr. Kramer went on. "I now have total confidence in you. I hope you'll both be with us for a long time."

"Fine with me," Joel replied.

"Me too," I agreed, "except it'll have to be part-time when school starts."

"Yes, I understand that," Mr. Kramer answered. "In fact, your honesty when you applied was one reason I hired you."

"Oh, he's real honest," Joel said, giving me a look. Naturally Mr. Kramer didn't catch the sarcasm.

"I'll let you get back to work now," Mr. Kramer decided. "By the way, did you have any trouble with the car, Sam?"

I frowned. "Trouble? No, none at all."

"Good. After you left, I remembered that the car you took doesn't have a spare tire," Mr. Kramer explained. "We'll see that it doesn't happen again."

Joel swallowed. "No spare?"

"I'm just glad you didn't have a flat," Mr. Kramer said with a smile. "That'll be all. Oh, let me have that routing sheet as soon as possible, Sam."

"Yes, sir," I agreed, quickly leaving the office. Joel was right behind me, though.

"Hey, Sam, wait up!" he whispered.

"Have to get that routing sheet," I replied, trying hard not to laugh.

"Did you know we didn't have a spare?" Joel wanted to know.

"No, of course not," I answered truthfully.

"Oh man, if I had told Kramer we had a flat and changed it ourselves. . . ."

"But you didn't," I reminded him. "I'd better get that routing sheet."

I hurried on to the parking lot, grinning all the way. Joel and his foolproof scheme! If I had given into temptation and gone along with it I would have been the fool. An unemployed one.

w w j d   p o w e r   s t a t e m e n t

To be stable is to be reliable and consistent in your behavior and actions so that you can be counted on.

s c r i p t u r e

You have been born again, and this new life did not come from something that dies, but from something that cannot die. You were born again through God's living message that continues forever.

1 PETER 1:23 NCV

Staying in Shape

By Mike Chapman

Mom was paying bills when I left the house. "And just where are you off to?" she asked.

"I have a date with a couple of dumbbells," I replied.

"Chris, that's no way to talk about your friends," she admonished.

"Mom, I'm going to work out," I answered, grinning and holding up my gym bag as proof.

"But you just got home from school," she said. "Didn't you work out there?"

"That was basketball practice," I said. "Now I'm going to lift weights," I explained. "See you later."

"If you expect to play on my team you'll get rid of the flab!" Coach Forrest had barked the first day of tryouts. He looked at us and shook his head.

"Frankly, most of you won't be able to take it, and that's fine with me. I only want the men who can."

Right then I decided I was going to be one of those "men" who made the team. When my arms were turning to jelly on the thirty-fourth push-up, I wasn't so sure, but seeing other guys collapsing all around me just convinced me to work harder.

"Is he a coach or a drill sergeant?" Jacob Winslow wheezed as we took a lap around the gym.

"This is good for us," I replied, even though my legs were telling me they were undergoing cruel and unusual punishment.

"Another lap!" the coach yelled.

There were groans, and some of the guys dropped out—but not me.

"I feel like I've been run over by a truck," Jacob complained on the way home. "How about you?"

"I'll live," I replied. "I'm gonna make the team too."

"Good luck," Jacob said. "Are you coming to Bible study tonight?"

"I'm too tired. I want to get to bed early so I'll be ready for tomorrow."

And I was ready the next day—unlike half of the guys who didn't show up for a second day of torture.

"We'll probably cut this number in half," Coach Forrest warned. "One! Two! One! Two! A little more enthusiasm, gentlemen!"

The muscles I had used the day before were screaming in pain, but I pushed myself. I was no quitter. Jacob wasn't either, I guess, because he was there too.

"You should have been in Bible study last night," he told me as we walked home. "We're starting a new project," Jacob went on. "We'll visit people who have visited the church and share Christ with them."

"Good. Guess we'll find out tomorrow—who made the team, I mean."

"Right," Jacob agreed. "Well, see you later. Think about joining us for the witnessing class."

"Yeah, sure," I said. But I didn't think about it. I was too busy thinking about making the team. My muscles may have been sore, but I kind of liked all the pressure I was putting on myself. Besides, I didn't need to attend a class to learn how to witness.

Jacob and I made the team, and I started putting more and more time into working out and getting in shape.

On one particular afternoon, the weight room at the fitness club was almost deserted. *What is this?* I wondered. There were a few of the older guys around, but hardly anybody my age.

"Excuse me," I said to one of the older guys. "Are you using these dumbbells?"

"Help yourself," he replied. He glanced at me. "You're in good shape for someone your age."

"Thanks," I said, feeling a little embarrassed. I took the weights to the nearest incline board.

"You know, Henry," I overheard that guy telling his friend, "I used to be built like that."

"So what happened?" Henry asked.

It was hard not to snicker. The first guy had a big potbelly and was obviously out of shape.

"Oh, I got the flu and then I got weak, and the weaker I got the less I felt like working out," the first man explained. "I figured I'd wait until I was feeling strong again."

You get stronger by working out, not waiting until you suddenly feel strong. I felt like telling them that. I was living proof too. I was really weak before Coach Forrest got ahold of me. But the more I worked out, the stronger I got.

I was doing some triceps extensions when Jacob finally showed up. "Can I work in?" he began.

"Okay," I answered. "Of course you'll have to reduce the weight a little."

"Very funny," he replied, starting to use the same weight I had been using. "Hey, you weren't kidding! I can barely budge it!"

I shrugged. "Told you so."

He did his set, then looked at me. "You have really gotten stronger the past couple of months."

"I've been working at it," I said simply. "Pays off."

"We've been missing you at church," he said

"I'm there every Sunday," I reminded him, starting another set.

"Yeah, but I'm talking about at Bible study and other stuff like that," Jacob continued. "You're missing out on most of the activities."

I finished my set. "There's only so much time in a day, you know. Your turn."

"I have a guy I want you to meet, Jacob told me. "He's new in my neighborhood, and he's a fan of yours," Jacob explained. "He's seen you play in a few basketball games. Why don't you come over to my place Saturday afternoon?" Jacob suggested. "We can play basketball, and you can meet Graham."

So I did. I was going to practice shooting baskets anyway, and it didn't really matter where I did it.

"Oh, I forgot to tell you," Jacob whispered when Graham went chasing a runaway ball down the driveway. "I've been inviting Graham to go to church, but he hasn't been too interested. Maybe if you invite him, he'll come."

"Yeah, okay," I agreed.

We played for a while longer; then Jacob's mom called us in for drinks.

"I have to make a phone call," Jacob said suddenly, giving me a look. "Be back in a few minutes."

So this is invite-the-guy-to-church time, I thought, not too thrilled about it. Still, it was no big deal. "What are you doing tomorrow?" I asked.

"Nothing much," Graham replied. "Why?"

"Why don't you go to church with me?" I said.

I guess I expected him to jump at the chance, since he was supposedly a fan of mine. But he didn't. "I don't think so," he answered. "I don't care anything about church. Why do you go?"

That stopped me for a second. Why did I go to church? I had never really thought about it; I just always went. "Well, to worship God," I managed. "I'm a Christian, Graham."

"So what does that mean?" he asked.

"What does it mean?" I repeated. "Well, I—I'm going to Heaven when I die and—" Suddenly my mind went totally blank, and I couldn't think of an answer.

"What if somebody doesn't believe in Heaven?" Graham asked.

There had been a time when I would've know the answer to that, but all I could do was stammer and stumble around until Jacob came back. I couldn't believe what I was hearing then. Jacob told Graham exactly how a person can receive Jesus as Savior.

"Where did you learn all that?" I questioned Jacob after Graham went home.

"In the witnessing class," Jacob explained. "I wish you'd start coming, Chris."

I wanted to tell him that I didn't have time, but I wouldn't let myself. I had as much time as anybody else; I just had to decide how to use it.

I may have been getting physically stronger with those extra workouts, but my Bible study and prayer time had really suffered. I was getting spiritually weaker all the time. My feeble attempt at witnessing to Graham had convinced me how out of shape I was—spiritually speaking, that is.

Give up the basketball team? No, it wasn't necessary to do that. But I sure made some changes in my priorities after that afternoon.

w w j d   p o w e r   s t a t e m e n t

Jesus was up against some rough competition but he stayed strong by staying in touch with his source of strength: God His Father. For us to become stronger as Christians, we too must stay close to the source.

s c r i p t u r e

*Finally, let the mighty strength of
the Lord make you strong.*

EPHESIANS 6:10 CEV

History

By Julie Durham

Anxiously, I looked at the clock. Only ten more minutes to freedom. Well, actually, it would be longer than that by the time I finished my sidework.

Since Christmas, I've been waitressing in a restaurant franchise. Thank heavens this is my last week. Actually, I don't dislike waitressing. Last summer, I loved working at a family-owned restaurant. But there's a world of difference between a family restaurant and a franchise.

One difference is the pressure. Most customers don't realize I have to be at their table with water within sixty seconds after they sit down. That can be difficult, especially if I'm detained by another customer.

In a franchise, everything is timed to the second. You have to deliver the meal in so many minutes and check within three minutes to make sure everything is okay. You have to refill drinks; promptly remove empty plates; and encourage dessert at the proper time.

Besides handling at least six tables, we have to prepare desserts, drinks and some of us—me included—work the register. We often have to bus our own tables and clean any messes. Before we can go home, we have to scrub our booths and refill all salt, pepper, ketchup, and sugar dispensers.

We also have to do "sidework." Sometimes it's cleaning freezers or straightening the storage room.

My least favorite is washing the restaurant windows. We also do "prep" work, like cutting pies and scooping butter into 200 little cups. What a pain!

And then there's rolling silverware. I think that's the worst job of all. We have to spread the napkin, place the spoon and fork on top of the knife just right, roll it a certain way, and slip it into a plastic sleeve. And we have to do 200 of these before we can leave!

With all the pressure, it's easy to get upset about little things, and tempers flare. Sometimes walking through the waitress line is like walking through a combat zone. I've had some good chances to share my faith simply because the Lord has helped me keep my temper.

Finally, my shift was over, my sidework done, and I could roll my silver. Angie finished at the same time and joined me. Normally Angie's kind of talkative, but she was quiet for a change. We go to school and church together, so we're pretty good friends. I've discovered if Angie is silent, you know there's a problem.

"Did you get good tips?" I cautiously asked.

"Not really." she sighed. "They're okay, but not nearly enough. I need to either make bigger tips or work more hours."

I was surprised. She's already working eight more hours than I am—and I work too much to keep up with school.

"Why?" I asked.

"I need to start paying for some more things around the house." Angie said tersely, then bit her lips as if to seal them. That was unusual, too. Angie is never secretive.

I noticed her fingers fumbling. Several times, she had to reroll her silver because it was too crooked to pass our manager's inspection. Then she accidentally hit the pile that was accumulating by her elbow. As it fell, the silverware slipped out of the napkins and clattered across the floor.

Usually Angie finds things like that hysterically funny. But this time, she just sat and began sobbing into a napkin.

"Don't worry. I'll help you roll more." I murmured, picking up silverware.

Still crying, she gulped, "Thanks" and started rolling again.

We worked in silence for a minute. Then I decided it was time to get to the heart of Angie's tears.

"I know something's wrong. Why don't you tell me about it?"

She licked a tear off her lip. "Just a rough day, I guess." She tried to smile, but more tears edged over her long black lashes.

"I have a feeling that it's more than that," I countered. "And I think you need to talk about it. After all, what are friends for?"

She hesitated—then dropped her silverware and looked at me.

"Julie, I'm so confused lately."

"About what?" I prompted, placing a knife in the center of a napkin.

"About everything. About life. It just doesn't seem worth living anymore."

I'd heard that those were words a person sometimes used when they were thinking about suicide. But surely not Angie—she was "Miss Perfect"—a great family, a nice home, good grades, a cheerleader, and besides that, a Christian. After all, Christians were never tempted to take their own lives . . . or were they?

"What makes you feel that way," I asked, searching for the right words.

"Everything." She said hopelessly. Then the words rushed together.

"My parents are fighting like crazy—the other night I heard them talking about going to a marriage counselor. Everyone I know whose parents have gone to a marriage counselor end up getting a divorce. If they do, I'll have to help mom support the boys. Julie, if they split up I'll go crazy.

"A lot of their fights are about my brother Jon. He's been taking drugs. Dad wants to make him go to a rehab center. Mom doesn't want to. I'm worried about Jon. He's changing. And Phil's only ten, but he idolizes Jon. I'm afraid he'll follow in Jon's footsteps."

I muttered something real intelligent, like "bummer," but Angie kept talking, almost like she'd forgotten I was there. She stuffed her rolled silver into the sleeve so ferociously that it broke right through the plastic.

"And I don't know what to do about Mike. He's acting really strange . . . I think he's going to break up with me. I just couldn't stand it without Mike. . . ."

She looked at me with pain-filled eyes. "I know it's wrong for a Christian to even think about, but lately I've been wondering if it'd just be easier to end it all—to down some pills and fall asleep forever. I don't know what to do. Everything just seems so . . . hopeless."

Whew! Not exactly the conversation I'd been expecting. I knew the best thing to do was listen, but something in Angie's tone made me realize I needed to say something—that she needed some reassurance. Just talking about her problems in itself, as I'd been learning in a peer counseling class, was a request for help.

Oh, God, I cried silently, *You know I've never dealt with someone who's talking about suicide. What in the world do I do?*

For a minute, it didn't seem like God would answer my plea. But then Angie's last word rang in my mind. *Hopeless.* Maybe that was the key—to help Angie see hope.

Still praying, I spread out another napkin and mechanically plunked a knife on it.

"Angie, sometimes work really stresses me out," I started. "It's hard when the cooks take too long and burn the meal; or your customers gripe, and the manager is yelling; or you get stiffed." I stuck my rolled silver in a bag. "I used to get really upset about things like that. I'd go home with my stomach tied in knots. Then one day, I realized it was really stupid. So what if it took me ninety seconds to get to a table or if someone had to wait a minute for their coffee? An hour later, they would have forgotten all about it. And within a few hours, I realized I'd be at home with it all behind me. When things went wrong, I had to learn to just do my best. And if something went wrong that I couldn't do anything about, I had to tell myself, *In a few hours, this will be history.*

"That helps me cope better. I start to see things in perspective. I realize that the things I'm worrying about at the moment will soon all be resolved—one way or the other. Problems don't hang on endlessly. And often, the things I worry about turn out fine.

"The stuff in your life right now isn't that easy. I know you're going through some difficult problems." I paused, groping for the words. "But maybe things won't turn out as badly as you expect. Maybe a marriage counselor will help your parents do better together. And a rehab center might help Jon conquer his problem. Maybe all the things you're sure will go wrong will go right after all. This time next week, all your worries of today just might be history. Suicide won't do anything to help the problems in your family—it'll just make it worse for everybody else. For your parents, Jon, and Phil. They need you to be a strength in their lives right now."

"I hadn't thought of that," she said. Her face was streaked with mascara rivulets. She wiped it off with a napkin and blew her nose.

We were quiet for a moment, then I added. "Once, Pastor Harris said something that really stuck with me. He said we should never make any serious decisions when we're going through a valley in our lives—especially not the decision to end it all. Valleys don't last forever, Angie. If you just hold on, maybe you'll find a mountaintop on the other side of the valley. Maybe you'll find out there was cause for hope after all."

"Maybe," she contemplated, straightening her silverware stack. "But Julie, I just can't seem to get rid of the thoughts. Sometimes I lie awake at night, so tempted to sneak my mom's sleeping pills. Why can't I shake those thoughts?"

I shrugged. "Look Angie, I'm no spiritual giant, but if there's really spiritual warfare in our lives, like the Bible says, those thoughts might stem from that. Maybe suicide is a temptation, like any other temptation. Maybe Satan's trying to induce you to end it all. Maybe because if you fight it and make it through this, he knows you'll be able to make a big impact for the Lord in someone's life—maybe even in your own family."

"A temptation, huh? I never thought of that before . . . ." The tears had finally stopped. Angie's brow puckered in thought. "So if it's a temptation, then I'd need to face it like any other temptation, huh?"

"Well, I haven't thought much about it," I admitted, "but I bet you're right."

We were quiet again for a few minutes. I didn't know if I'd been any help to Angie, or if she just wrote off my words as a lecture. After a few minutes, she completely changed the subject. We began talking about school, then about the party our youth group is having next Friday night. Finally, I won't have to work and will be able to go to a youth group party again! We speculated about whether or not Matt will ask me to go with him—he's been hanging around me a lot lately.

"I've nearly become a wreck wondering if he's going to ask me to it or not!" I exclaimed. Then, by Angie's reply, I knew that some of my words had sunk in, and that maybe God had been able to use me.

She gave me a mischievous grin as she replied, "Well either way, this time next week, it will be history!"

w w j d   p o w e r   s t a t e m e n t

We are not capable of solving all of our problems. There are many things that are out of our control and bigger than we are. But none of them are bigger than God. Fortunately, in a world where our pain can be so deep, our hope is not in ourselves: it is in the God we serve.

s c r i p t u r e

God began doing a good work in you,
and I am sure he will continue it until
it is finished when Jesus Christ comes again.

PHILIPPIANS 1:6 NCV

Overheard in the Locker Room

By Walt Carter

Chad Carter was one guy I couldn't figure out. He was really friendly and everything the first time I went to his church, so we became good buddies right away.

Or so I thought.

We went to the same high school and didn't have any classes together, but I'd still see him in the hall once in a while. That's when his behavior really bothered me.

"Hey, Chad!" I'd yell. "How're you doing?"

He'd just sort of nod and hurry on. At first I figured he was late for class, but nobody's in a hurry all the time—unless it's on purpose.

Chad avoided me in the cafeteria too. I was almost sure of it. I actually saw him duck behind a post in an attempt to keep me from seeing him, or lean over to pick up a non-existent spoon which had supposedly fallen to the floor.

Only once did we spend lunch hour together, and that was at the beginning of the fall semester. I had known him for just a week or two then. The coaches had a noon sports program set up, and anybody who wanted to play flag football could come out. Chad and I decided to try it after we finished lunch one day. It would've been fun, I guess, but I got on a team with some guys who didn't know a thing about football. Chad was on the team, too.

I'll have to admit I got really mad a few times during the game. I had been working on it but still blew up occasionally, and when I blew up I said a lot of things I shouldn't have. But I always cooled off pretty fast.

When the game was over and we went to the locker room to dress, I couldn't find Chad anywhere. It was like he had vanished. From then on, we just hardly ever spent any time together at school.

At church it was just the opposite. We got along great and talked and laughed like the buddies I thought we were.

"I'll meet you for lunch tomorrow," I'd suggest just before leaving church on Sunday.

"Uh, no," he'd answer quickly. "I can't. See you, Rick."

Of course I had a lot of friends at school—most of whom weren't Christians and didn't go to church, much less believe in Jesus—so I didn't usually think about Chad and how weird our relationship was, unless I saw him.

It could be my imagination, I thought, as he conveniently disappeared into a classroom seconds before we would've passed each other in the hall. It was possible that he really had a class in there, after all. Then I glanced at the room number and frowned. It was Miss Fitch's room; she taught sewing and nutrition!

I continued on down the hall but didn't leave the building. There was a janitor's closet next to the library. I stepped inside, leaving the door open just a crack. From there I could see almost the entire corridor, including Miss Fitch's room, but nobody could see me.

I didn't have to wait long. Chad, looking slightly embarrassed, came out of the room and continued on down the hall in the same direction he had been going previously. As far as I was concerned, that was enough evidence. Chad was definitely avoiding me! But why?

Maybe I should've just called him up and asked him, but I would've felt stupid. I decided to try an experiment instead. It might force Chad to tell me; anyway, it was worth a try.

I was waiting when Chad got to school the next day. It was early and I stationed myself at his locker. He saw me when he entered the building and paused momentarily, as if deciding what to do. Then he came toward me. The hall was nearly deserted.

"Hi, Chad!" I called out, smiling.

"Hi, Rick," he replied when he was close enough to speak without raising his voice. He opened his locker, put in some books, and took out a couple others. "I'll see you," he told me, closing the locker. "I have to go to the library and do some reading for a book report." He turned away.

"That's okay," I answered. "I'll go with you."

He seemed very aware that the halls were rapidly filling with other kids. "Anybody can use the library," he said, "but there's no talking allowed."

We started down the hall together, but not really together at all. It was as if Chad was pretending I wasn't with him. He'd answer my questions with a grunt or a nod.

"What'd you do last night?" I asked finally.

"Went to youth group at church," he said, getting the words out as fast as he could.

I was looking at Chad as he spoke—even though he wasn't looking at me—and didn't see Greg Reardon coming down the hall. Of course Greg takes up about the whole hall. He banged right into me, sending books and notes and everything else I had been carrying, crashing to the floor.

"Why don't you look where you're going, you jerk!" I yelled. I said a few other things too, which I won't repeat.

When I got my books and other stuff together, Chad was nowhere around. I didn't find him in the library, either.

As much as I tried, I didn't see Chad for the next couple of days. When I did see him on Friday, he and some other kids from church were together in the quad, talking.

"What's going on?" I asked.

"We are talking about starting an early morning prayer group," one of the girls told me. "So we're going to circulate petitions and everything," she went on, ignoring the looks Chad was giving her. "We even have these signs ready to use to advertise."

"I'll carry a sign." I picked up one that read, "Prayer Group, Tuesday mornings."

"Uh, thanks anyway," Chad said quickly, taking the sign out of my hand. "We-uh-we have all the people we need."

"Okay, then I'll take some flyers," I offered.

The other kids, except for the one girl who was new to our church, had funny expressions on their faces. Chad led me away from the group.

"I don't know exactly how to say this," he began, "but we don't want your help, Rick."

I frowned. "What are you talking about? I go to church. Why shouldn't I help?"

"You can help by leaving us alone," he went on. "Let me explain—"

I began to boil inside when he said that. Apparently I didn't live up to his expectations of what a Christian was supposed to be! That was obviously why he had avoided me like I had a disease!

"Carter, I'm sick of your—"

The principal arrived on the scene at that particular moment, so our conversation was cut short.

It wasn't until I was in fifth period that I started thinking about what Chad had told me. Who'd he think he was, anyway? It wasn't just Chad, either. All those church kids gave me weird looks when I volunteered to carry a sign or pass out flyers.

I swallowed as my anger gave way to puzzlement. Why would they treat another Christian like that? It didn't make sense.

After school I stopped by the boys' locker room to get my gym clothes. I was tying them up in a bundle when some other boys came into the locker room. They went to a locker in an aisle closer to the door, so they didn't even know I was in the room.

"Did you see those church kids trying to get attention for their prayer group?" one voice asked.

"Yeah," the second voice replied. "The principal stopped that pretty fast!"

"I thought I saw Rick Harmon with them," the first voice said.

"No, I think he was just arguing with that Chad kid," the second voice answered. "Imagine Harmon in church!" They both laughed. "He has the worst temper of anybody I know," the first voice went on, "and the worst mouth!"

"You're telling me?" the second voice questioned. "I've seen and heard him in action a couple dozen times—like the other day when Reardon accidentally bumped into him in the hall. Maybe he does go to church; he uses God's name enough!"

The first voice laughed. "Yeah! Let's go."

I sat there for a while after they left. Was that why Chad stayed away from me? Did my reputation embarrass him? And was that why he and the others didn't want me associated with the prayer group?

But I don't swear that much! I told myself. I swallowed. It wasn't true. Of course any would've been too much. And the second something went wrong, I'd express myself, usually using God's name plus a few other choice expressions. *But I always asked the Lord to forgive me afterwards*, I reminded myself.

227

I had never committed the problem to God, though, or asked Him to control my mouth. Maybe I even refused to admit that it was a problem. Suddenly I knew better.

A guy's locker room may seem like a strange place to pray, but I bowed my head right then and there and surrendered my temper to Him. It was a step in the right direction.

Later I told Chad about what I had done. He was glad, of course, and admitted that he probably hadn't handled the situation the way he should have, avoiding me instead of just telling me. But he was afraid to tell me. I did have a rotten temper. That's past tense. With God's help I'll keep it that way.

w w j d   p o w e r   s t a t e m e n t

There's an old adage that says "you can never not communicate." Your choice of vocabulary says much more than the words themselves. It tells others what kind of person you really are and what you truly value. If you care about what is noble and good, then your speech will reflect it.

s c r i p t u r e

Watch the way you talk. Let nothing foul or dirty come out of your mouth. Say only what helps, each word a gift.

EPHESIANS 4:29

My Mind Went Blank

By Alan Cliburn

It was Michelle Marsden's fault. Well, not really, but if she had been sitting up straight I probably never would have done it.

Cheated, I mean.

Okay, so I wasn't ready for the test. I admit that, but I still didn't plan to cheat. I mean, it wasn't as if I told Michelle to lean to the left while she was writing her answers or anything like that. She just did.

Even then I didn't think about copying what she wrote down. I didn't do stuff like that; I was a Christian who knew better. Sure, there had been a time when I wouldn't have given it a second thought. But when I accepted Christ a year ago, I decided to really live for Him, and that meant changing a few things in my life.

Of course this was different. The reason I wasn't ready for the test in the first place was because of church. Well, sort of anyway. I mean somebody had to volunteer to make posters to announce our next youth group activity, and God had given me a fair amount of artistic talent.

"Where's Dan?" I asked when I got to church. He was an even better artist than I was.

"Had to study for a test," Renee Kellogg replied. "He has Mrs. Quinlan for history and her tests are really monsters."

"Yeah, I know," I agreed. "I have her this semester, too. In fact Dan's in my class."

"Then what are you doing here, Aaron?" the youth director wanted to know. "Are you ready for that test?"

"Not really," I admitted. "But I can study when I get home."

The youth pastor got a phone call about then, so Renee, Mark, and I went to work on the posters. Nobody else showed up, so it took until about 9:00 P.M. to finish them all.

I didn't go straight home after we finished the posters either. Renee and Mark said they were going out for a pizza, so I decided to go along. "All that work made me hungry," I explained.

"But if you have that test tomorrow—" Renee began.

"We aren't going to stay at the pizza place all night, are we?" I asked.

"No, in fact the shorter the better," Mark replied. "I want to practice my speech for debate when I get home."

Renee and I talked him into practicing on us while we were eating. It didn't take much persuasion. I guess time just got away from us. It was 11:30 by the time I got home, and I was dead tired.

I planned to get up early and do some last minute studying before school, but that never worked for me. And especially if I had been up later than usual the night before. As it was, I got to school just as the bell rang for first hour.

"Missed you last night," I whispered to Dan as I passed his desk. "We got the posters made, though."

"Guess I'm not as good in history as you are," he replied.

"Let's get started," Mrs. Quinlan began in that take-charge voice of hers.

I was okay until I looked at the first question on the test. She was asking for battle philosophies as well as dates. Battle philosophies? My mind went blank. I glanced over the other questions, looking for an easy one. There were none. Evidently the answers were all in chapter eleven, a chapter I had never actually read.

I checked out the rest of the room. Nearly everybody was busy writing, including Dan. Paul Desmond and I were probably the only ones in the whole class who didn't know what to put down. Paul just shrugged when our eyes met briefly.

Michelle sure has nice handwriting, I thought suddenly. Easy to read, too. Before I knew what was happening, I was reading her answers, then rewriting them on my paper, except I'd change a few words around, of course. My heart was pounding so loud that I was surprised nobody sitting near me heard it, but I kept right on copying her work. Cheating. I couldn't believe that I would do anything like that, but that didn't stop me.

"Time!" Mrs. Quinlan announced as I dotted my final "i."

I sat there like a zombie as she collected the papers and reminded us of our next assignment; it was almost as if I was outside myself looking in, and I didn't like what I saw.

What did you do? I demanded of myself, at once full of guilt and shame. All those arguments which had seemed so logical when I was in the act of copying Michelle's answers fell apart as the full impact of what I had done hit me.

God, forgive me! I prayed silently as I left the building and headed for the spot where some of the church kids met for lunch. I stopped before I got there, though. I didn't feel like being around anybody right then. Besides, I felt sick to my stomach.

So what are you going to do? I wondered. What could I do? There was no way I could un-cheat, after all, and I had already asked to be forgiven.

"Hey, that was pretty clever, Hesterman," a voice began.

I glanced around to see Paul Desmond standing by a tree, hands in his pockets. "What are you talking about?" I asked, frowning.

"I'm not blind," he said. "I saw you eyeballing Michelle's paper during the test."

"Paul—"

"Listen, don't worry," he went on. "I'm keeping my mouth shut. Everything's cool."

"Everything isn't cool," I corrected. "In fact, I'm on my way to tell Mrs. Quinlan what I did right now."

"You're crazy!" he informed me, mouth open. "Why would you do anything stupid like that?"

"Because cheating was stupid," I explained. "I don't know what made me do it, but I'm telling Mrs. Quinlan."

Paul looked at me disgustedly. "I always thought you were weird, but now I'm sure of it. Does this have anything to do with your religion?"

"I'm a Christian, if that's what you mean, and Christians don't go around cheating on tests."

"Yeah, but you did," he reminded me.

"That doesn't mean I'm perfect," I answered. Right now I have to catch Mrs. Quinlan before she leaves for lunch."

"Yeah, you do that," Paul advised, stalking off toward the cafeteria.

Paul didn't seem too impressed by my honesty or the reason for it. Maybe later he'd think it over and be curious about my decision to confess.

There was no way of knowing, of course. I didn't even know what Mrs. Quinlan's reaction would be. There was no doubt in my own mind that I was doing the right thing. I guess a Christian always knows what's right, though, if he's honest with himself and with the Lord.

Of course knowing and doing are two different things.

w w j d   p o w e r   s t a t e m e n t

God's Word says that we will never be tempted beyond what we can bear. You always have access to the power of God to say "no" to temptation.

s c r i p t u r e

Take everything the Master has set out for you,
well-made weapons of the best materials.
And put them to use so you will be able to
stand up to everything the Devil throws your way.

EPHESIANS 6:11

From Tragedy to Triumph

By Cindy Wainwright

The suitcase was lying in the middle of the living room rug when I dashed into the house. Suddenly I forgot all about telling Mom that her brilliant, talented daughter had passed algebra.

It was a black suitcase, old and battered, and the identification tag read "Mrs. Gayle Perkins." Then it gave Aunt Gayle's address in Fairmount.

I put my books down quietly and listened for voices. There were none.

"Mom?" I called out apprehensively. "I-I'm home."

Then a door opened and closed in the hall and Aunt Gayle appeared, a finger to her lips. "Shhh," she whispered, "your mom's resting."

I swallowed. "But Aunt Gayle," I began softly, unable to stop myself, "what's wrong? Mom was okay when I went to school this morning. She was fine."

"It's too early to tell," Aunt Gayle said. "She collapsed right after lunch. Luckily your father was here. He called me."

"Is there anything I can do?" I wanted to know.

"Pray, honey," she answered simply.

Mom was feeling better that night and wanted to get up, but Aunt Gayle and Dad insisted she stay in bed. I had a feeling they knew more than they were telling me. I was fifteen; I had a right to know what was going on. After all, she was my mother. I confronted Dad while Aunt Gayle was doing the dishes.

He looked at me with tired, swollen eyes and suddenly I didn't want to know whatever he knew. He led me into the den and closed the door.

"Only very basic tests have been made so far," he told me. "At the hospital tomorrow—"

"The hospital!" I interrupted. "Daddy—what's wrong?"

"Dr. Reimers believes your mother may have cancer, Bethany."

I was momentarily paralyzed.

"We didn't want to tell you until it was definite," Dad went on. "She'll spend several days in the hospital while tests are conducted."

"But Mom's always been so healthy," I began, swallowing.

"Not all cancer is terminal, honey," Dad reminded me.

"I know," I answered, forcing a smile. "Maybe with surgery she'll be fine."

"That's the spirit," he said. "Now you'd better run help your Aunt Gayle with the dishes.

I nodded as I hurried out of the den. But I didn't go right to the kitchen. I couldn't. Tears filled my eyes and wanted to spill down my cheeks. I had been able to hold them back while I was with Dad, but now I cried silently, so Mom wouldn't hear. I went into the bathroom and washed my face with cold water.

Right there in the bathroom, my face still wet, I asked God to help my mom. At first it was formal, like I always prayed. I had asked Jesus to come into my heart when I was eight, but being a Christian had always been so casual and natural that I took it—and Him—for granted.

In the weeks that followed I grew up a lot. Mom did have cancer, and it was serious; but she wasn't "at death's door," or anything like that. She was able to be up and around, and Aunt Gayle went back home.

My own prayer life became a real source of strength and communication. I could feel the love of God in my life. It brought our whole family closer together.

Several months later, the black suitcase again greeted my return from school. Aunt Gayle was in the kitchen, preparing supper.

"Where's Mom?" I asked cautiously.

"In the hospital, honey," Aunt Gayle replied. "She broke her legs today."

I thought I was ready for anything but the news caught me off guard. I stared at my aunt. "Both of them?"

"I don't understand it, either," she said. "Your father is there now. I'm sure he'll explain everything when he comes home."

Dad looked exhausted when he came in an hour later.

"What is it?" I wanted to know. "How did she break her legs?"

"The cancer has spread to her bones," he said. "She'll be bedridden the rest of her life. We need to pray."

I didn't feel like praying; I felt like crying. But I bowed my head and closed my eyes and listened as

Dad started talking to God. It was a simple prayer. He asked God to be with Mom, of course, and for us to be able to accept whatever happened as His will.

It didn't make sense to me. How could it be God's will for Mom to have cancer? I talked to Dad about it later.

He put an arm around me and shook his head. "I don't pretend to know why things happen the way they do, honey. But I do know that Romans 8:28 says 'And we know that all things work together for good to them that love God, to them who are the called according to His purpose' (KJV). Mom is trusting in the Lord completely. That's all we can do."

I learned to be cheerful around Mom—even when she broke her legs a second time—and most of the time I really felt it. We had a relationship that few of my friends had with their parents.

Mom came to my high school graduation in a wheelchair. She was smiling and radiant, a real testimony to some of my non-Christian classmates who knew of her illness.

I moved right into the college group at church. It wasn't long before I heard about their outreach program, where they'd put on a musical program and then individually talk to members of the audience about Christ. I was all for it until I found out that we would be gone for nearly five days. That stopped me. Mom was growing weaker. I couldn't be away from her for that long.

But when Mom heard about the trip, she wanted to know why I wasn't going. Eventually she got it out of me, and then insisted that I go. I did, and it was one of the most rewarding experiences of my life. Three months passed, and our group went on another evangelical outreach trip. There was no question that I would go.

If this were fiction instead of fact, I suppose Mom would have suddenly begun to improve. But it didn't work out that way at all. As the end of summer approached, she grew much weaker. There were many nights when we thought she was gone.

At the same time, the college group was planning its final trip before the fall semester began. I think everyone at church was surprised when I signed up— Mom had been on the prayer list for weeks. But I knew Mom wanted me to go.

Almost from the beginning it was obvious that this would be the most effective outreach project our group had attempted. It was well planned, we were well trained, and the community was backing us one hundred per cent.

I had said good-bye to Mom Friday before we left, of course, but I didn't realize that it would be for the final time. Halfway through that weekend I received a call from Dad. Mom had died.

Of course it was a blow, I'd be lying if I said otherwise, but I felt peace and serenity inside, too— peace and serenity that only a Christian can have at such a tragic moment. I remained with the church group for the entire weekend, instead of rushing home. I knew I could do nothing at home, but there was much to be done for Christ in the little resort town where we were staying. I had the opportunity to witness to many more kids before the weekend was over.

But the most wonderful thing happened Sunday night. The woman who had opened her home to five of the girls from our church—me included—came to our final musical program. When Stella, the guitar player, spoke to her afterward, that woman asked Jesus to come into her life and save her soul.

"The girl whose mother died has something I want," she told Stella, referring to me.

I had stopped questioning why Mom had to have cancer a long time ago and learned to trust that God is always in control.

w w j d   p o w e r   s t a t e m e n t

When tragedies happen, it's okay to cry. Remember that when Jesus lost friends He loved, He expressed His grief and pain. Sometimes there are no words to take the pain away. But, like Jesus, we are to place our faith solely in God and bring our wounded hearts to Him.

s c r i p t u r e

You're blessed when you feel you've lost what is most dear to you. Only then can you be embraced by the One most dear to you.

MATTHEW 5:4

Lessons from a Firefly

By Julie Berens

The sound of laughter drifted through the open window where Jenalyn O'Connor lay on her bed staring at the ceiling. She knew it was her little brother, Bobby, and his friend, D.J., out on a firefly expedition.

"I wish my biggest problem was catching lightning bugs," Jenalyn said to the stuffed tiger at the foot of her bed. "Why does life have to get so hard when you turn fifteen?"

The tiger just stared back at her. *Typical,* Jenalyn thought. *No one has any answers for me—except Mom. She's got my life all mapped out.*

As much as Jenalyn loved her mom, she didn't love her mom's plans for her future.

"I've heard of boys carrying on in their father's footsteps," Jenalyn had told her best friend April just a few days ago, "but not of girls following in their mother's. Just because my mom always wanted to be a nurse doesn't mean I want to be one. She talks about nursing like it's her ministry or something."

"With all the people she helps, I'm sure it is," April had replied. "Anyway, Jena, your mom's not a mind reader. If you don't want to be a nurse, tell her. She'll understand."

Jenalyn wasn't so sure. With a mom and two sisters who were nurses, Jenalyn felt like she'd be a traitor if

240

she said she was more interested in helping out at summer kindergarten camp than working at the hospital. Besides, being a candystriper, becoming an R.N., and working at Providence Hospital was a family tradition. It was planned. It was expected. But it was not what Jenalyn wanted to do with her life. Working at the kindergarten camp for the summer and becoming a teacher was.

In fact, Jenalyn had been helping out at a kindergarten class for a couple of months now as part of a special program at school. Since her last class was study hall, Jenalyn was dismissed early to work with the younger kids.

It was there she'd met Tanika and discovered that by drawing silly pictures she could get the little girl to talk and laugh when no one else could. And then there were Garrett and Simon. They loved the game she invented where she would draw a part of an animal and then add other parts until one of the boys would guess what the animal was. Mrs. Shaw, the kindergarten teacher, had remarked how good she was with the kids.

A knock on the door interrupted her thoughts. Even before the door opened, Jenalyn knew it was her mom leaving for work.

"Everything's set for you to start at the hospital," Mrs. O'Connor said as she came to sit on the corner of Jenalyn's bed. "I even picked up your uniform for you."

Jenalyn couldn't think of anything to say, so she just nodded.

"We're going to have such fun together, Jenalyn," her mom continued. "I'll show you around, and we can have lunch together. It'll be just like when your sisters were candystripers. I know you'll love nursing and helping other people as much as we all do."

"Sure, Mom," Jenalyn said without enthusiasm.

"Anything you need to talk to me about, honey?" Mrs. O'Connor asked, pushing back Jenalyn's bangs. Jenalyn opened her mouth to tell her mom about the kindergarten camp, but when she saw the look in her mom's eyes, she stopped. She didn't want to put out the light of the dream she saw there. "No, Mom," she said, "everything's great."

When her mom left, Jenalyn got off the bed and went to the window. She pulled back her curtain and stared at the stars. "Lord, I don't know what to do," she whispered. "I don't want to disappoint my mom, but I don't even like the thought of being a nurse. Hospitals depress me." She sighed. "I really like helping out at kindergarten—especially with Tanika."

She stared at the small white lights in the sky. "But then there's all that stuff about honoring your parents. My mom has always dreamed her girls would be nurses. Trisha and Betsy are. Am I supposed to, too?" She paused, waiting for an answer. "If I am, could You have one of those stars blink twice for 'yes' and three times for 'no'?" Jenalyn continued to stare at the sky, but nothing happened. "I didn't think so."

"Hey, Jena, come on down and count our lightning bugs," Bobby shouted. He and D.J. held up their jars for inspection. The fireflies fluttered about, blinking on and off.

"Not now, Bobby. I'm busy," she called back.

"Bobby, it's late. Time to get ready for bed," Jenalyn heard her mom call from the back deck.

Bobby and D.J. said their good-byes and headed inside. Next, Jenalyn heard the pounding of Bobby's feet on the stairs and then her brother burst into her room.

"You need more light in here," Bobby said as he came to the window with his jar of fireflies. "Good thing I brought these for you." He handed Jenalyn the jar. Its yellow glow brightened the room just a little. "Mom said I need a bath, so will you watch these? She said no glass in the bathroom." He was gone before she could reply.

Jenalyn looked in the jar. Fifteen fireflies. Not bad for a night's work. "Okay, bugs, blink twice for 'yes' and three times for 'no,'" she said with a smile. Her smile disappeared as the light in the jar grew dimmer.

Even with the holes poked in the lid, Jenalyn didn't think the fireflies would survive the night. They weren't meant to be bottled up so Bobby could scare away shadows in his room with "nature's nightlights" as he called them. They were supposed to be flying around outside.

Suddenly the fireflies lit again, and Jenalyn was startled to see the reflection of her face in the glass. It looked like she was caught in the jar with the bugs. As the light in the jar dimmed again, a small light inside of Jenalyn began to burn brighter.

"Being cooped up in this jar isn't why God created you," Jenalyn said. "Just like being cooped up in a hospital doing a job I'd hate isn't why God created me." She wanted to unscrew the jar lid and let the bugs fly out of her open window right now, but she knew that wouldn't be fair to Bobby. She also knew that taking the job as a candy striper at the hospital wouldn't be fair to herself or her mom. She had to follow the light of her own dream, not someone else's.

Cradling the jar of fireflies under her arm, she headed downstairs to talk to her mom. She'd talk to Bobby about letting them go, but right now she wanted to show the lightning bugs to her mom and explain about feeling trapped in a dream that wasn't her own. She'd tell her mom about Tanika and Garrett and Simon too—about how it felt to help other people and the joy it brought her. As she walked, she said a prayer that her mom would understand—about the fireflies, about breaking tradition, about following a new light, about the joy of a dream set free.

w w j d   p o w e r   s t a t e m e n t

Truth is more than just confessing when you have done something wrong. It means being true to the person that God made you to be.

s c r i p t u r e

But when the Spirit of truth comes, he will lead you into all truth. . . . he will speak only what he hears, and he will tell you what is to come.

JOHN 16:13 NCV

Louder Than Words

By Cindy Wainwright

I heard the news about Keren while I was washing out beakers for Mr. Coleman in the science lab after school.

"Come on, Maya, let's go," Gracie Martin said, sticking her head inside the door. "Pew! What's that awful smell?"

"We did an experiment with sulfur today," I replied. "It always smells like this."

"How come you have to clean up?" Gracie wanted to know. Then she nodded knowingly. "Don't tell me—you volunteered. Right?"

"You said not to tell you," I reminded her. "But somebody had to do it, and Mr. Coleman went to a faculty meeting."

"Maya, have you ever wondered what would happen if you didn't do all the things you do?" Gracie asked.

I blushed slightly. "I don't do so much."

"I think people take advantage of you," Gracie went on, "and what do you get out of it anyway?"

"Christians are supposed to help others," I began. "Don't you remember how Jesus washed His disciples' feet?"

"Oh, that reminds me!" Gracie exclaimed. "Keren Duncan's a Christian!"

I stared at Gracie in disbelief. "Keren? But how? When?"

245

"I don't know any of the details," Gracie admitted. "Look, I can't take this smell another second or I'll pass out. I'll wait for you outside."

"Don't bother, I'm not going straight home," I replied. "I have to stop by Mrs. Hamilton's house and do her laundry. Her arthritis is acting up again."

"Maya!"

"See you at church tonight," I said.

"Okay," Gracie agreed, a disgusted look on her face.

Keren Duncan a Christian! I thought as I rinsed out the last few beakers. It was hard to believe. She was one of the most popular girls in school and always seemed to be so self-satisfied.

I didn't know her very well, even though we lived in the same neighborhood and had several classes together. Her friends were members of the student council and that type; mine were less well known around school, people like Gracie who kept out of the spotlight.

"You should invite Keren to come to youth group," someone had suggested to me once. "She may be pretty, but that doesn't change her spiritual condition."

I knew that was true and would've been glad to invite Keren to our youth group—or even share my personal testimony with her—but I couldn't. I was so shy that I barely said anything at all unless I knew the other person really well.

So someone else had to invite Keren. I think Carla Winters finally did, because Keren came several times with her. Carla was so outgoing that she probably kept witnessing to Keren until it sunk in, I decided.

The air was cool and crisp as I hurried toward Mrs. Hamilton's little house. It was just a block from the school and she was always glad to see me. I felt the same way about her.

I hadn't been helping with her laundry and other chores very long. I didn't even realize she was there and needed help until the youth pastor told about this senior citizen in our church who could use some assistance.

"She was a teacher in our Sunday school until her arthritis prevented her from regular attendance," he added. "Any volunteers?"

No one else raised a hand, so I did, keeping it up just long enough for the youth pastor to see it.

I arrived at home from Mrs. Hamilton's just as Mom was fixing dinner. "Maya, would you mind taking a pot of soup over to Mr. Bigelow? He hasn't been well, and his wife is in the hospital."

Keren and her father were getting out of the car when I passed their house on my way to Mr. Bigelow's tiny cottage on the corner.

"Hi, Maya!" Keren sang out.

"Hi," I replied.

"Could I talk to you for a second?" she asked.

"I'll stop on my way back," I promised. "I have to get this soup to Mr. Bigelow while it's hot."

I rang the bell when I reached the cottage, but he didn't answer. "Mr. Bigelow!" I called.

When there was no response, I tried the door. It was unlocked. *Maybe he really is sick,* I thought, suddenly concerned. I opened the door and walked inside. "Mr. Bigelow?"

I heard a muffled groan and then saw him, lying on the living room rug. "Help me!" he whispered hoarsely.

The phone was out of order, so I raced out the front door. Keren and her father were still unloading groceries from their car.

"It's Mr. Bigelow!" I called. "Come quick!"

In a matter of minutes an ambulance had been called and was on its way.

"Thank goodness you were home," I told Keren and her father as the ambulance attendants were loading Mr. Bigelow onto the stretcher. "I don't know what I would've done if you hadn't been."

"But we don't deserve any credit," Keren insisted. "If you hadn't brought that soup over here he could've been there for days without anyone finding him."

"Maybe," I agreed. "Right now I'd better fix something to eat."

Keren frowned. "You mean here? But if Mr. and Mrs. Bigelow are both in the hospital, who—"

I answered her question by pointing at a furry face peeking out from under the couch.

"A kitten!" Keren exclaimed.

"There are four of them," I said. "Not counting the mother cat. And they're probably all hungry."

"Can I help you feed them?" Keren asked.

"Okay," I agreed. "Come on."

We found an ample supply of cat food, and all four kittens—plus their mother—appeared in the doorway at the sound of the can opener.

"I'll put everything away when they're finished," I told Keren. "You can go if you want."

"Not yet," Keren replied. "I have something I want to tell you. Remember I wanted to talk to you later?"

"I almost forgot," I admitted. "With all the excitement, I mean."

Keren smiled. "I wanted you to know that I'm a Christian now."

I nearly told her I already knew, but changed my mind. "That's wonderful, Keren! I'm sure you'll never regret it."

"I'm sure I won't, either," she said.

"I know Carla must be thrilled," I went on.

"Carla?" Keren repeated. "I don't think she knows. She was absent today, and I haven't had a chance to call her."

"But I just assumed that she was the one who led you to the Lord," I explained, frowning slightly.

"Well, she certainly did have a lot to do with it," Keren agreed. "She took me to church and youth group and told me what being a Christian was all about. Your pastor made the steps necessary to accept Jesus very clear."

I nodded. "Then your decision was based on what a lot of people said, not just one."

Keren smiled. "No, it was mostly because of one person, Maya. And it had nothing to do with what she said, because she didn't say anything!"

I shook my head. "I don't know who you mean."

"I mean you!" Keren exclaimed, laughing,

I stared at her, mouth open. "Me? But I—"

"I used to go to Sunday school when I was little," Keren went on. "That was before we moved here. The thing I remembered most about Jesus from the stories we heard was that He helped people and wanted to do things for others. But most of the so-called Christians I knew only cared about themselves."

She obviously wanted to talk, so I remained silent. Besides, I was still in a state of shock.

"When I saw you at youth group that first night, you volunteered to help some old lady with her housework. I thought that was beautiful. I've been watching you a lot since then, Maya, even though you weren't aware of it. You're always doing things for people and never get, or even expect, credit for it!"

"Doing things for other people can be its own reward," I said simply, a little embarrassed.

"Anyway, I wanted what you have, and that's why I asked Jesus to come into my heart last night," Keren told me. "So thank you very much, Maya."

I wanted to speak, but couldn't right then. With that big lump in my throat I could barely smile. Still I knew that Keren got the message.

wwjd power statement

People are watching you. You are a walking, talking, living, breathing testimony for Jesus every day as you go to school or work or hang out at home.

scripture

A good person gives life to others;
the wise person teaches others how to live.

PROVERBS 11:30 NCV

Worrywart

By Teresa Cleary

Erin Fulton stood in line at the grocery store and glanced at her watch. She sighed. She'd never get to her older sister's house by 3:30. She'd told Betsy she would pick up diapers for four-month-old Nathan, but she hadn't expected it to take so long.

"Hurry up, hurry up, hurry up!" she said under her breath to the lady in front of her who was digging in her purse for a nickel. Erin checked her watch again and moaned. It was already 3:45. Fifteen minutes less to talk to Betsy and there was so much to tell her.

Finally the lady found her nickel and moved through the line. Erin quickly paid for the diapers and hurried out to her bike. She pedaled as fast as she could while holding the diapers in one hand and steering with the other.

Erin parked her bike against the side of Betsy's garage and raced to the back door. Through the window she saw Betsy bouncing Nathan, while a bottle heated on the stove.

"Come on in, Erin!" Betsy called over Nathan's cries. "I have my hands full!"

"Sorry I'm late," Erin said, setting the diapers down on the table. "Hope you weren't worried."

"No," Betsy said with a smile. "I figured you got stuck at school or the lines at the store were horrible, as usual. Besides, you're the worrywart in the family, not me."

Erin had to admit her sister was right. She was notorious for worrying about everything.

Before Betsy had gotten married and the family still took vacations together, Erin was always the one who asked Dad if they had enough gas or if he was obeying the speed limit so that they didn't get pulled over. In fact, whenever there was a problem in the family, someone was sure to quip, "Let Erin worry about it."

Erin sat down at the table. "Well, if you'd heard Dad and Mom talking last night, you'd be worried too."

Betsy took the bottle from the stove, tested the milk, and gave it to Nathan. His crying stopped.

"Wish my problems could be solved that fast," Erin sighed.

Betsy sat down next to her sister. "Okay, what's up? What are you worried about now?"

"Dad was talking about work last night and he told Mom they're laying people off in June. One hundred engineers will lose their jobs and he might be one of them."

Erin stood up and paced the kitchen. "If Dad loses his job, we'll probably have to move. That means I'll have to say good-bye to my friends, good-bye to you, Tom, and Nathan, and good-bye to any chance of being captain of the drill team next year."

"You forgot good-bye to the youth group," Betsy said without a smile, but with a twinkle in her eyes.

"It's not funny, Betsy," Erin wailed. "My world is falling apart, and you're joking about it."

"Sorry Erin, but I think you're overreacting." Betsy put Nathan over her shoulder to burp him. "I know there are problems at the factory, but Dad has more seniority than most guys there. Layoffs won't happen until June. That's three months away, and you've already got yourself tied up in knots."

"I can't help it," Erin moaned. "I'm a born worrier. You know that. Whether it's Monday's project, Thursday's tryout, or Friday's test, I start worrying about it ahead of time. That way I'm prepared."

"You gotta stop it, Erin, or you'll end up with an ulcer or warts or something," Betsy told her.

"Warts?"

"Yeah," Betsy laughed. "Worry warts!"

"Real funny," Erin said, her temper flaring, "but tell me you never worry. When you look at all the crime and drugs in the world and then you look at Nathan, tell me you don't worry about him."

Betsy shook her head. "Am I concerned? Yes. Worried? No. Those problems may be bigger than I can handle, but they're not bigger than God."

Betsy put Nathan in his swing and walked over to where her Bible lay on the counter.

"Don't quote me Matthew 6," Erin said. "Dad and Mom do it so much I know the verses by heart."

She recited in a squeaky voice, "Therefore I tell you, do not worry about your life, what you will eat or drink; or about your body, what you will wear. Is not life more important than food, and the body more important than clothes? Look at the birds of the air; they do not sow or reap or store away in barns, and yet your heavenly Father feeds them. Are you not much more valuable than they? Who of you by worrying can add a single hour to his life? . . . Therefore do not worry about tomorrow, for tomorrow will worry about itself (Matthew 6:25-27, 34 NIV.)

"Brilliant, Erin," Betsy said, giving her sister a hug. "You've memorized the verses; now what are you going to do about them?"

"What am I supposed to do?" Erin said, moving away from her sister and flinging her hands into the air.

"I think something like that would be very effective," Betsy replied.

"Like what?" Erin thought her sister must have gone nuts. Betsy threw her hands in the air as dramatically as Erin had. "Give your worries away," she said.

"Yeah, like someone else wants my problems," Erin retorted. She shook her head. She'd come to Betsy for help, and instead she was more frustrated than before.

"Look, I gotta go," she said. "Mom's probably putting dinner on the table, and I don't want her to wor—"

Betsy smiled slightly. "I'll call and tell her you're on your way. Thanks for getting the diapers. Your money is on the counter."

Erin kissed Nathan and stomped out the back door. She hoped the ride home would clear her head, but even the wind rushing by her ears seemed to whisper, "Worry!"

Later that night, Erin sat on her bed with her Bible open. *What am I supposed to do, Lord?* she thought. She smiled as she remembered Betsy's response. "Give your worries away," her sister had told her.

Even though Erin had dismissed that advice, she hadn't forgotten it. In her mind she began to replay all her worries—real and imagined. After she'd thought of everything she could, she clenched her hands into fists like she was actually grabbing all those worries.

Lord, I usually try to handle all my problems on my own, Erin admitted. *I realize now, I can't handle any of them without Your help, so I give them to You.* Erin opened her fists and raised them to heaven.

At first she felt a sense of peace; then almost as quickly as she had sensed her worries disappear, she felt them creeping back into the corners of her mind.

I guess I'm not very good at this yet, Lord, she admitted.

But then another thought pushed back the worries. *Do not worry about tomorrow. . . .*

"All I can do is my best," Erin said aloud to herself. "That's all the Lord wants."

She almost laughed. "And it's not like I have to do this alone. God will be there to help," she said, "because He loves me—Erin Fulton—worry warts and all."

w w j d   p o w e r   s t a t e m e n t
Worry is evidence of a lack of trust. Take all of the things you are worried about today and place them in the hands of the God Who loves you completely. He can be trusted.

s c r i p t u r e
Do not worry about anything, but pray and ask God for everything you need. And when you pray, always give thanks. And God's peace which is so great we cannot understand it, will keep your hearts and minds in Christ Jesus.

PHILIPPIANS 4:6-7 NCV

Additional copies of this book and
other titles in the *WWJD* series
are available from your local bookstore.

WWJD for Kidz

WWJD Pocket Bible

Answers to WWJD

Answers to WWJD Journal

Honor Books
Tulsa, Oklahoma